A Handbook of Th␣␣␣␣␣for Social Care:

Volume One

By: Siobhan Maclean

Kirwin Maclean Associates

City & Guilds name and logo are the registered trade marks of the City and Guilds of London Institute and are used under licence.

"City and Guilds logo © City & Guilds 2002"

Whilst the publisher has taken all reasonable care in the preparation of this book the publisher makes no representation, express or implied, with regard to the accuracy of the information contained in this book. Neither the publisher nor the City and Guilds of London Institute accept any legal responsibility or liability for any errors or omissions from the book or the consequences thereof.

A Handbook of Theory for Social Care: Volume One
Siobhan Maclean

First published 2006 by Kirwin Maclean Associates
First Edition 2006: ISBN-10:   1-903575-42-7
ISBN-13:   978-1-903575-42-0

A catalogue record for this book will be available from the British Library.

©*Kirwin Maclean Associates, 47 Albion Street, Rugeley, Staffs*
All rights Reserved

Printed in Great Britain

CONTENTS

THEORY AND PRACTICE: AN INTRODUCTION

Don't be intimidated by the word theory. Theories in social care are nothing more than an attempt to explain social relationships. Theories have been developed since it became clear that there were similar patterns or repeating cycles of behaviour both in an individual's life and in the lives of lots of different people.

Since theories have been expressed by academics and social scientists, they often use an academic language. Don't let that put you off. Theories are life dressed up! Many theories actually have a very simple message. Einstein who developed what is probably the most famous theory of all – the theory of relativity – said:

"A theory is the more impressive the greater is the simplicity of it's premises, the more different are the kinds of things it relates to and the more extended the range of it's applicability."

(www.thinkexist.com 2005)

There has been some debate about what actually constitutes a theory. Generally, a theory helps to explain a situation and perhaps how it came about. In science a theory is seen as helping to:

- describe (eg: what is happening?)
- explain (eg: why is it happening?)
- predict (eg: what is likely to happen next?)

Whilst individual social care theories have different purposes, using all kinds of theory in our work offers us, as social care workers, some important things:

- Theories can help us to make sense of a situation. Using theory, we can generate ideas about what is going on, why things are as they are etc.
- Using theory can help to justify actions and explain practice to service users, carers and society in general. The aim is that this will lead to social care becoming more widely accountable and ultimately more respected.
- In work with individuals, making use of the theories which may relate to their specific situation will give us more direction in our work with them.

- Using theory can give a reason about why an action resulted in a particular consequence. This can help us review and possibly change our practice in an attempt to make the consequences more effective.

It is clear then, that theory is important in practice – both for work with service users and for social care to be more valued in society.

Some people will claim that they don't use theories, but that they work on common sense principles. But whose sense is common? Is your sense the same as everyone else's? Just because someone cannot imagine another way to view something doesn't mean that they aren't using theory. It just means that their one or two theories are their entire world or "sense".

There is an old saying, started by Leonardo Da Vinci, "Practice without theory is to sail an unchartered sea; theory without practice is not to set sail at all." Imagine a boat setting out to sea in a good breeze, without a map or compass. This is like practice without theory – how will the crew know when they have arrived at their destination? If they do (by a remote chance) arrive safely in a port they like, how would they ever be able to repeat the journey? On the other hand, a boat might bob along tied to it's bollard, safely in the harbour. It might well have every direction finding device known, but isn't going anywhere. This is like theory without practice. It's pointless.

As well as describing some of the key theories that are used in social care, this book will also discuss some of the models that relate to social care. Models are less developed than theories but are also intended to describe and explain. Models often have a less scientific or research based grounding but they do appear to offer some insight.

This book is one of two in a series. Both are intended as introductions to the way theory can be applied to social care. This volume is intended for direct care and support staff. Volume two in the series is intended for managers and students on the first year of a social work or social care degree.

SECTION ONE: OPPRESSION AND ANTI-OPPRESSIVE PRACTICE

This section begins by defining some of the key words in this area. It moves on to explore some of the main theories about oppression and how and why it occurs. It concludes by exploring some of the theories about challenging oppression and working in an anti-oppressive way.

Reading this section, you will learn more about:

- Values
- Oppression
- Discrimination
- Marginalisation
- Internalisation
- Prejudice
- Social imagery
- Stereotyping
- Labelling
- Equality
- Diversity
- Anti-oppressive Practice

THE VALUE BASE

The issues covered in this section are often covered by the term "the value base". This term and the word "values" is in common usage in social care. To a lay person the word "value" conjures up images of bargain hunting or financial efficiency in services. However, in terms of social care, the value base is essentially about a code of conduct that defines the way in which staff should work with people.

The word values could be replaced by the word "beliefs". What we *value* is what we believe is important.

Personal Values

It is generally accepted that personal values are influenced by a number of factors. The factors which influence and shape our personal value system might include:

- Our background and upbringing (often referred to as socialisation)
- Personal experiences
- Education
- Religious beliefs
- Cultural background

Because we are all individuals and the above factors will be different for everyone, then all individuals have a different set of personal values.

Professional Values

Every organisation has values – these are usually expressed through organisational codes and standards. In addition, social care has a value base – which is expressed in the code of practice for social care.

Whilst the professional value base does not replace each individual's personal value base, professional values do over-ride personal values in terms of the way in which staff work with people. Staff must adhere to the professional value base. Essentially when we go to work, we should leave our personal values at home.

Value Conflicts

The subject of values is complex and conflicts often arise. This is sometimes as a natural consequence of meeting new experiences and situations. In order to deal with dilemmas and conflicts in a professional manner, it is important to recognise conflicts in values and work constructively to resolve them.

> Mary is a home care worker. As a result of her background, upbringing and religious beliefs Mary has strong personal opinions about gay relationships. She views them as "morally wrong and abnormal". One night she is supporting a service user at home. In the background the television is on and a soap opera depicts two men kissing. The service user says "that shouldn't be allowed on telly. It's disgusting." Mary feels torn to agree but knows she should uphold people's rights and choices as part of the professional value base.

Values and Anti-oppressive Practice

An awareness of values in social care is essential to, and an integral part of, good practice. The following framework for anti-oppressive practice, outlined by Dalrymple and Burke (1995) highlights the vital part that values play in this process:

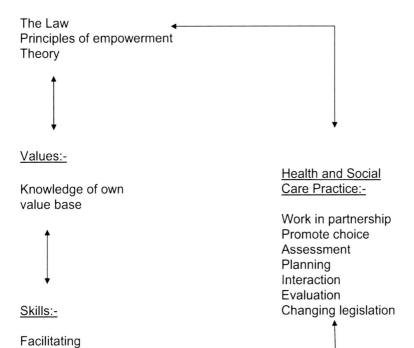

Knowledge of:-

The Law
Principles of empowerment
Theory

Values:-

Knowledge of own
value base

Skills:-

Facilitating
Advocating
Negotiating

Health and Social
Care Practice:-

Work in partnership
Promote choice
Assessment
Planning
Interaction
Evaluation
Changing legislation

This diagram shows that what we consider to be important will shape the way in which we work. If we feel that it is important to work in partnership and to promote choice then we will develop skills that enable us to pursue this e.g. facilitating, advocating etc. If we consider that upholding rights is important then we will develop knowledge around law and the rights that people have while receiving services, etc.

It also demonstrates that good practice is made up of three vital components – knowledge, values and skills. The knowledge and skills that people need will vary with each individual's role and responsibilities. However, the values needed to work in social care are common to all care workers (ie. the value base of social care). What will be different is our own personal values and it is vital to be aware of these in order to work effectively within a social care environment.

OPPRESSION AND ANTI-OPPRESSIVE PRACTICE

One very clear definition of anti-oppressive practice is outlined by the Inner London Probation Service (1993). They state that anti-oppressive practice:-

"exposes, challenges and seeks to replace forms of oppression which lead to discrimination, and marginalisation."

Clearly, it is therefore vital to have an understanding of the main types of oppression, and the ways in which it is manifest. It is important to begin by looking at definitions of some of the key words in this area.

Prejudice

This is where an individual makes a judgement based on either inadequate or inaccurate information which leads to the development of irrational preferences. Prejudice is based on ignorance or misunderstanding. One of the main features of prejudice is rigidity or inflexibility of ideas. This means that new information may not have an impact on prejudicial views.

Marginalisation

Marginalisation is a process where people who are not valued within society are excluded from the mainstream of society. For example, it is difficult for people with disabilities to access many employment opportunities.

Discrimination

This does have a definition within the law. A brief definition however, would be treating somebody less favourably, for example, on the grounds of their gender, sexuality, race, disability etc.

Oppression

The root of the word oppression is the latin word "opprimere", which literally means to press down or to press against. This is very relevant to oppression, which is about "squashing" people and treating people in a way which stops them growing and developing (Philipson 1992). Oppression is often used as an "umbrella" term covering all aspects of discrimination.

Internalisation

Oppression is a very powerful force. The impact of the negative experiences of oppression can result in feelings of worthlessness and lower self esteem. People actually begin to believe and adapt to the messages conveyed (sometimes on an unconscious level). This process is referred to as "internalisation" and can result, amongst other things, in despondency and dependency.

Who is Oppressed?

Most people will have been oppressed in some way, at some stage of their life. However, it is widely accepted that some groups of people are more likely to be oppressed than others. For example, Black people, women, people with learning disabilities etc. Some of the main forms of oppression which have been identified in British society are outlined in the following box.

- **Racism is basically discrimination based on differences arising from people's ethnicity. The nature of racism and understanding of it has changed and developed over the years.**

- **Ageism is the term used to describe the discrimination faced by older people on the basis of their age.**

- **Disablism is the word used to cover the oppression faced by people with disabilities.**

- **Sexism covers discrimination on the basis of gender. In British Society, the word sexism is usually used to described the oppression faced by women.**

Other less well known terms are:

- Adultism – this describes the discrimination faced by children and young people.

- Classism – this describes oppression based on class differentials. Because oppression is so linked to power and it is those who are more powerful who oppress, this word is usually used to describe oppression faced by working class people.

- Heterosexism – this describes the oppression faced by gay people.

There are many other forms of oppression, which don't necessarily have a specific name or term. For example there are no commonly accepted words to describe the oppression faced by people with learning disabilities or mental health problems, homeless people, drug users, homeless people etc.

Doubly Disadvantaged?

When looking at who is oppressed, it is important to remember that oppression is a complex process. Many people will be oppressed because of more than one characteristic. For example, Black people with a learning disability will be subject to racism as well as discrimination based on their learning disabilities. This complex process is often known as double discrimination (oppression based on two characteristics) or triple jeopardy (oppression based on three characteristics).

Types of Oppression

It is commonly accepted that there are three main types of oppression – individual, institutional and structural and these can be either covert or overt:

Individual Oppression

This is where the actions and attitudes (often unconscious) of individuals towards marginalised groups support and sustain a broader social pattern of discrimination.

For example, a man might believe that women should be responsible for all household chores and childcare. The way this man acts towards women will sustain the broader view of women in society.

Institutional Oppression

This is where institutions (for example: schools, churches, residential services etc) in reflecting the structure of the society they serve, maintain a set of rules, procedures and practices which operate in such a way as to perpetuate discrimination against marginalised groups.

Structural Oppression

This is where oppressive institutions work together, such that a structural or societal system of oppression is generated and sustained.

For example, people with a learning disability face oppression from all the major institutions within our society, such that they are segregated within education, employment and housing, etc. Furthermore they receive inadequate treatment within the legal framework, judicial system and health service. The list goes on…….

It is important to note that individual, institutional and structural oppression are very closely linked. After all, institutions are made up of a number of individuals. Therefore, individual beliefs and actions will have a profound impact upon organisations, institutions and society as a whole. The key to the difference however, is that where the oppression is carried out by one or two people this is individual oppression. Where the root of the oppression is in an organisation this is institutional oppression.

Overt and Covert Oppression

Oppression can be described as either overt or covert. Overt oppression is obvious or "open" oppression and therefore relatively easy to identify. Covert oppression is hidden, covered, oppression and can be more difficult to identify.

Mechanisms of Oppression

This is a term in common usage in social care. The term mechanisms of oppression refers to the systems or structures used to oppress people.

There are many mechanisms of oppression. For example:-

- Language
- Media
- Stereotyping
- Education
- Employment/unemployment
- Legal systems (laws etc)
- Health care
- Trivialising (eg: Jokes)
- Blaming the victim
- Labelling

You may be able to think of, and consider, more. Many of the mechanisms of oppression are explored in a theoretical approach referred to as social imagery or social constructionism.

SOCIAL IMAGERY

Social imagery is really about the portrayal of people who are often devalued by society. It relates to a whole range of areas, such as:

- Media
- Use of language
- Posters/Pictures/Décor within services
- Names of services
- Use of names for people in receipt of services
- How people dress etc.

To help understand the relevance of social imagery, we have explored some of these areas in this chapter.

Media

The media is very powerful in our society and promotes all sorts of images in a range of ways. For example, people with mental health problems are very often portrayed as dangerous in the media – particularly within newspaper headlines.

To look at the media in more detail, think about the service user group you work with – people with learning disabilities, teenagers, older people, homeless people etc – and then over the next few weeks watch out for any references to this group in newspapers, magazines, on the TV or radio, in films etc. Consider things like:

- What words/phrases are used to describe the group of people?
- Are these words/phrases positive or negative?
- How are people portrayed?
- Is this positive or negative?

You are likely to find that people are largely portrayed fairly negatively, or that the group of people you work with are mostly ignored within the media, which in itself gives an "image".

If you belonged to a group of people who were either continually ignored within the media or who were largely negatively portrayed within the media, this is likely to have a negative impact on your self image and hence your self esteem. Positive imagery is much more likely to have a positive effect on your self esteem and identity.

Use of Language

You may feel that as an individual social care worker you can have little impact on media imagery. However, you can apply the importance of social imagery to your own direct practice in a number of ways. For example, you can think about the images portrayed in the language you use.

To begin to look at this area, read through these two poems:

Tomorrow I am Going to Re-Write the English Language

I will discard all those striving ambulist metaphors
Of power and success
And construct new images to describe my strength.
My new, different strength.

Then I won't have to feel dependent
Because I can't Stand On My Own Two Feet
And I will refuse to feel a failure
Because I didn't Stay One Step Ahead.

I won't feel inadequate
When I don't Stand Up for Myself
Or illogical because I cannot
Just Take It One Step At a Time.

I will make them understand that it is a very male way
To describe the world
All this Walking Tall
And Making Great Strides.

Yes, tomorrow I am going to re-write the English Language.
Creating the world in my own image.
Mine will be gentler, more womanly way
To describe my progress.
I will wheel, cover and encircle.

Lois Keith, Cited in J Morris (1989)

Who is coloured?

When I was born
I was black,
When I grew up
I was black.
When I get hot
I am black,
When I get cold
I am black.
When I get sick
I am black,
When I die

I am black.

When you are born
you are pink,
When you grow up
you are white.
When you get hot
you go red,
When you get cold
you go blue.
When you get sick
you go purple,
When you die
you go green.

BUT YET YOU HAVE THE CHEEK TO CALL ME COLOURED!

Donna Davis

What are your thoughts about the messages portrayed in these poems?

A great deal is written about the power of language and that we should think carefully about the language we use.

General Guidelines

As a general rule, you should avoid terms which:-

Exclude – e.g. "Every man for himself" – "Standing on your own two feet"

Depersonalise – e.g. "the elderly, the disabled" etc

Stigmatise – e.g. "blackleg" – "black day" etc.

The following list is by no means exhaustive, but hopefully will enable us to begin to think about this area, and put thought into our communication via language.

Discriminatory	*Anti-Discriminatory*
Man, mankind	People, humankind etc.
To man/man-hours etc	To staff, to cover etc.

Chairman	Chair, Chairperson
A black mood	Bad mood
A black day	A bad day, a terrible day
Black (in the sense of dirty)	Dirty, grubby
The disabled	People with disabilities or disabled people
The elderly	Older people, elders
Mental Handicap	Learning disability
Mixed race/half caste	Of dual heritage
To a man	Everyone, everybody
Fireman	Firefighter
Policeman	Police officer
One man show	One person show
Coloured	Black

Add as many others to the list as you wish.

It is important to continue to think about your use of language. Use the following points to prompt you as an ongoing checklist:-

- Does the use of this word/phrase label people in a negative way?
- Does this use of language undermine people's strengths?
- Does this use of language depersonalise others, stereotype them etc?
- Does this use of language devalue the individual/group?
- Does this use of language patronise?
- Facilitate positive images for all.
- Don't make assumptions that because one person/group has indicated a preference for certain words/phrases this will be shared by all.
- Treat the opportunity to learn about the use of language as an adventure in gaining new knowledge and understanding.

> In a day service for people with multiple disabilities, it is common practice for staff to refer to lunch time as "feeding time" and a "feeding rota" is put in the kitchen to show who staff should be assisting with their meal. Soriya recognises that this language is very negative, particularly in terms of social imagery and she sees it as contributing to stereotyping and oppression. She raises the use of language in her next supervision session.

Service Décor

Many services have realised the impact that service décor has on how services are viewed and have tried to maintain a good physical environment. There are still some exceptions. Examples include some day centres which have uncarpeted corridors and a communal wall with loads of coat hooks. By comparison most offices are carpeted throughout and office workers keep their coats either in their own room or close to them.

Names of Services

As the saying goes "There's a lot in a name." The names given to services very often have 'images' attached. For example, very many older peoples homes are called things like "Greenfields." "Green Meadows"....? It sounds as though people are being put out to pasture! Swimming Clubs for people with disabilities are often called names like "Dolphins" or "Penguins". This gives a childlike impression as opposed to "Burtonwood Swimming Club".

Many national organisations have changed their names or the names of individual service provision because of the importance of social imagery.

Social imagery should not be under-estimated. It can be belittled and minimised by reference to the term "political correctness". However, generally people using this term are not devalued people who are affected by social imagery and oppression more generally.

As one of the main mechanisms of oppression, social imagery feeds into the processes of stereotyping and labelling.

STEREOTYPING

Stereotyping is the process of people ascribing set characteristics (generally negative) towards all or most members of certain groups of people.

Neil Thompson (1998) has described stereotyping as having various characteristics. Stereotypes:

- are resistant to change even in the face of evidence which conflicts with the stereotype

- are largely negative
- become so established that they are accepted as reality without serious question.

Thompson points out that stereotypes are transmitted both by individuals and by culture. They confirm, validate and entrench societal inequalities, since the stereotype is applied to a whole group or section of society.

A number of writers including Wolfensberger (eg: 1972) have identified that various common themes emerge in the stereotyping process and that people subjected to stereotypes are given a social role or category.

The Person as Subhuman-Animal or Vegetable (Wolfensberger) or Dehumanisation (Thompson)

Whilst this may appear extreme, it is an incredibly common process. Chattel slavery was justified on the basis that Black people were subhuman. Black people, people with learning disabilities and people with mental health problems have all had animal images closely associated with them. The use of aversive punishments, e.g. hitting, electric shock, denial of food etc, is probably rooted in this. People who enter very deep comas can be labelled as in a persistent vegetative state; some of these people have then had all medication and food withdrawn.

Thompson focused on the way language is the means by which dehumanisation occurs. People who are discriminated against are at risk of being entirely described by a label eg 'alcoholic', 'prostitute' etc.

The Person as a Menace (Wolfensberger)

Many people who are devalued within society are considered a threat or as a potential criminal. Additionally, as a group, people can be seen as a social threat to the well-being of society. For example, people with mental health problems are often portrayed as dangerous in the media.

The Person as an Object of Dread (Wolfensberger)

This is related to the two previous characteristics. The person is seen as a dreadful entity or event. Associated with this is the medieval concept of the person as a "changeling". This can be seen in the way people with mental health problems could be described and in the way parents, who have been informed that their new born child has a learning disability, are described as grieving for the child they never had.

The Person as an Object of Pity or Burden of Charity (Wolfensberger) or Welfarism (Thompson)

The person may be viewed as being subject to misfortune for which they bear no responsibility and who therefore requires special attention or services. The pitied person will be seen as blameless for the situation they find themselves in and perhaps therefore unaccountable for their actions.

Where there is no compassion, only a sense of duty, the person will be seen as a burden of charity. Whilst the person may be entitled to basic necessities, they are not entitled to anything considered luxuries, frills or extras. The recipient of such charity is expected to be grateful and, as far as possible, to work for their 'keep'.

Thompson (1998) uses the term welfarism. This refers to the situation where certain groups are seen as in need of state welfare support through health or social care services. Thompson makes the following points about welfarism.

- It is stereotypical; all individuals within a group are assumed to rely on state welfare despite evidence to the contrary
- It is demeaning and patronising
- It creates dependency and erodes rights
- It reinforces discriminatory viewpoints eg. people are seen as a social burden and drain on the economy

The Person as a Sick or a Diseased Organism (Wolfensberger) or Medicalisation (Thompson)

The person is labelled as sick or a patient; they receive a diagnosis, and are given treatment or therapy, by doctors, nurses, paramedics or therapists which is intended to lead to a cure. The person may be entitled to the privileges, as well as subject to the demands, that are characteristics of the sick role generally. Privileges include exemption from normal social responsibilities, and recognition that the condition is not the individual's fault; the demands are that the individual must want to get well or at least better, and must seek suitable and appropriate remedy for their condition.

Many people in receipt of services are involved in activities which are classified as therapy, e.g. art therapy, aromatherapy etc.

Thompson (1998) goes on to develop and outline the additional effects on a person who is characterised as intrinsically 'ill'. These consequences include:

- Invalid status. A person who is sick is treated as an invalid – they are no longer a valid person. The person loses some degree of status whilst ill.
- Welfarism. The act of labelling as ill attracts welfare responses with a focus on care and not rights.
- Medical discourse and power. People who are viewed as ill are then placed in the domain of health professionals. Doctors and health professionals exercise significant power within a context that characterises them as the experts.

The Person as an Object of Ridicule (Wolfensberger) or Trivialisation (Thompson)

The person is not taken seriously and is the butt of jokes at their expense. Historically Black people have been depicted by the media as servants or light entertainers. People with learning disabilities have been characterised as the village idiot.

Thompson recognises the point that Wolfensberger originally made. Additionally, Thompson argues that the process of trivialisation is used to undermine anti-oppressive practice. The example given by Thompson (1998) is where discussions about sexism are hijacked by discussions focusing on whether a man should hold open a door for a woman. Reference is also made to the way the term 'politically correct' has been coined to dismiss issues of language and anti-oppressive practice.

　　　　　　　　　　　copyright© Kirwin Maclean Associates

The Person as an Eternal Child (Wolfensberger) or Infantilisation (Thompson)

People with a learning disability are particularly at risk of being viewed as a child, although people with physical disabilities and older people can also be. When a person is so viewed no strong or even reasonable adaptational demands are placed upon the person. There is no expectation that the person can accept adult responsibilities and rights.

Thompson's use of the term infantilisation closely follows the meaning of Wolfensberger eternal child. Thompson (1998) highlights the way language conveys this, for example older people when they enter care or health settings 'lose' their name and staff use pet names (duck, love) as adults do with children.

The Person as a Holy Innocent (Wolfensberger)

The person is accorded religious characteristics. S/he may be perceived as incapable of consciously or voluntarily committing evil or malicious acts. Whilst this is probably the most benign social role perception, the danger is that people so viewed will be also considered as "other worldly" and not interested in ordinary human activity.

Invisibilisation (Thompson)

This refers to the process by which various groups of people are not represented in language or the media. Language has historically been male dominated and has used male terms for roles that could easily be gender free eg: Chairman.

Media images are noted for focusing on the dominant groups in society and by doing so ignoring other groups (making them invisible). Examples of this include the way older people, people with disabilities and people who are poor are significantly under represented in the media.

Marginalisation (Thompson)

Certain groups of people are pushed to the margins of society, they are excluded from the decision making process and the operation of power in general.

Examples of marginalisation include the way people with disabilities have been educated in 'special schools' and the way speakers of minority languages can find that their first language is pushed to the fringe.

> **Andrew started work at a residential service. Recognising the very low proportion of Asian residents in the service, he raises the issue at a team meeting. He is told "Well Asian people look after their own. Don't they?" Andrew recognises this as stereotyping and oppressive and decides to raise the issue in supervision to take things further.**

LABELLING

Labelling is the process by which a negative blanket term is applied to a person. The effect on other people, when they view that person, is to have a prejudiced and negative view which adversely influences their behaviour towards that person. The effect on the person, both of the label and of other peoples actions to them result in the person feeling judged and undermines their confidence. The person who is labelled may then act in ways that are a distortion of their true identity but, to the observer, result in confirming the validity of the label.

We all have labels given to us. A few people are fortunate enough to have the label of 'celebrity' or 'aristocrat'. Many of us have the label of worker or professional or student, partner, parent etc. Most of these labels are seen positively.

There are some labels that are negative and are not claimed by a person but are put on them by others. In social care, one of the problems is most of the service users are given labels by professionals. In origin the intention by professionals is not to give someone a negative label but to recognise that a person has identifiable special needs. Unfortunately many of the labels that professionals apply to service users are not neutral. Within society they are used negatively.

Social care services and health services continue to use labels because it is the principle means they use to identify who should receive certain services.

Hence there are benefits and disadvantages of having labels. Some of these are:

Benefits of Labelling

1.   Having a recognised label can explain a characteristic of a person. If a child is struggling with reading and writing at school they may be at risk of being 'labelled' lazy or slow etc. If the child is then assessed and found to have dyslexia, this can be a relief (in part) for the child and parents in that it explains why the child is having difficulties.

2.   Having a specific label should enable the person to receive specialist services that are able to meet the person's needs.

3.   Some professionals find it beneficial to label an individual. If the professional is working with a group of children or service users and one of them is presenting them with needs that demand more of their time and attention then by having the child or service user labelled it can result in the professional being given additional staff support or the service user is moved to a group of individuals who have similar needs.

4.   On a similar vein, organisations can benefit from labelling individuals if it results in being able to claim additional funds.

5.   Most statutory services for adults can only offer support to a person if they have a disability, mental health problem, are frail or infirm due to their age or have other support needs (eg an addiction to drugs or alcohol). Therefore there is a requirement to give a person one of these labels if they are to receive services.

In childrens services, a child has to be a 'child in need'. The definition of a 'child in need' is potentially quite broad but in practice services narrow the definition (to reduce demand on limited resources).

Disadvantages of Labelling

1.   The labels used by professionals are not neutral. They are nearly all viewed in society as negative. Some of the labels have a very significant stigma associated with them. The strength of this stigma should not be overlooked by those of us who are not given one of these labels.

2.   The label given by health and social care professionals to service users is often related to perceived 'deficits' of the

person. The labelling process is an indirect way of saying the person is incompetent (in one respect or another).

3.   The label may have originally had some meaning and purpose. However, it can quickly become misused and the person who has the label applied to them quickly becomes covered by it as if covered by a blanket. The label becomes the person's identity and almost their name eg. 'schizophrenic', 'alcoholic', 'epileptic' etc. When an 'ic' is attached to the end of a label, it is a sign that the persons individuality and identity has been lost under this label. Even without the 'ic', people can have their identity lost eg. "She's a hair puller!"

4.   As noted by Wolfensberger the label becomes a self fulfilling prophecy. If a person is given a negative label then health and social care staff are likely to be influenced by this and their behaviour could be different. If a person is given the label of 'aggressive' then staff may stand at more of a distance, be cooler in their whole approach and maybe have a colleague present. This could result in the service user recognising that a label has been applied to them and resenting the label. The service user is angry about the label, but this gets viewed by staff as confirming the claim that the service user is aggressive.

5.   Service users have no control over their label. It is passed to new staff by experienced staff. At one time or another, many of us have done something that could result in us being given a negative label. We manage to bury or lose the negative label. In Britain, by the age of 30, about 30% of men have a criminal record. Most men don't introduce themselves to someone new by saying "Hi, I'm Dominic, I've got a conviction for reckless driving. Do you want a lift home?" Most of us bury or lose our negative label by changing friends, moving etc and by not telling our new friends about our past. In services the label gets passed on, sometimes it is one of the first things a new staff member learns about a service user. Sometimes this label is inaccurate or exaggerated or it relates to an event that happened years ago. There are lots of ways to describe a person but too often the negative labels are passed on to the new staff very early in their working life.

By now you should have a good understanding of the way oppression works and you should have some ideas about how the service users you work with are affected by oppression. To give a broad overview, it is worth exploring some of the common experiences oppressed people can face.

EXPERIENCES	EXAMPLES
Rejection Kept at a distance from others. Placed with people in similar situations.	Segregated services keep people away from the general population and in groups of people with similar needs.
Diminished Experiences Less experience of different people, different places, different activities.	Devalued people may not be able to mix with the general population, activities may be limited etc, this is particularly so if people are in segregated services.
Low Expectations People have limited expectations of what devalued people can achieve.	A classic example is when people often ask a question to someone who is with a person in a wheelchair, rather than the person themselves "Does he take sugar?"
Loss People who are devalued often experience significant loss in their lives.	As a result of the negative experiences people will experience a loss of power, control, choice, rights, dignity etc.
Being seen as one of many Many people are not viewed as an individual, but as a label, or a condition or a problem.	Many people who are in receipt of services are viewed as a group. For example, going out in a group, the needs of the group over-riding individual needs etc. The general population may view people as a label, etc.

EXPERIENCES	EXAMPLES
Artificial Relationships A loss of real friends and contacts may lead to peoples' social networks being limited to paid staff and volunteers.	Many people living in residential services, or people who attend day services, are expected to rely upon other service users and staff to make up their social network.
Poverty People who are devalued are often reliant on benefits or trapped in poverty.	The weekly allowance of people living in residential care would not keep most people in the general population, even if all their daily living expenses (bill food etc) were paid for.
Labels People are often ascribed very negative labels.	In the general population, people are referred to by very negative labels or terms – eg. "mad" "handicapped". Within services people may be labelled as "manipulative, attention seeking, etc"

Working in an anti-oppressive way is essentially about breaking what is sometimes referred to as the "cycle of oppression" and altering many of these experiences.

EQUALITY AND DIVERSITY

Equality is a word often used in social care. Asked what this means, many people will talk about treating everyone in the same way. However, this is not equality – all of us, as individuals, are unique. However, for many reasons (many of which have been covered in this section) people who are oppressed are very often not viewed as individuals but as one of a group of people. Diversity, which is essentially about "differentness" is therefore vital. Equality or equal opportunities is not about treating everyone the same – almost the opposite; it's about recognising that everyone is different but ensuring that everyone has access to positive opportunities.

There are a number of ways to promote equality or work in what is often referred to as an anti-oppressive way. These include:

- Challenging oppression
- Recognising, responding and celebrating diversity (or differentness)
- Implementing approaches such as advocacy and empowerment
- Focussing on service user's strengths (sometimes referred to as the strengths model)
- Avoiding using oppressive practices such as labelling and stereotyping
- Understanding and challenging your own values.

In order to implement these strategies, it is vital to understand oppression and how it operates, which is why this forms the main focus of this section. To conclude this section, we are going to focus on challenging oppression.

<u>Challenging Oppression</u>

Whenever you come across a situation of oppression which you feel you want (or need) to challenge you should ask yourselves Why? What? Who? How? and When?

Why challenge?
It is important to challenge instances of oppression/oppressive practice because we all have a commitment to question and combat oppression in all its forms. Through challenging we are able to ask questions about oppression and oppressive practices which otherwise remain unnoticed.

What are you challenging?
Be clear about exactly what you are challenging. Listen, examine the issue, think about the context etc. Make the links with institutional oppression and structural forces. Working in this way, we avoid making challenging personally threatening.

Who are you challenging?
Ask yourself about the person you are challenging. It is our view that we should never avoid challenging because of the individual, but clearly we will need to alter the focus and content of our challenge based on the understanding and experiences of the individual. Think about communication in terms of the individual you are challenging.

How are you going to challenge?
You should choose the right way of challenging instances of oppression. You need to put thought into this. However we suggest you consider the following:

- *Understanding*
There could be a difference in what you understand and what the person you are challenging understands.

- *Values*
There may be a difference between what is important to you and what is important to the person you are challenging.

- *Styles*
There may well be a difference in the way you do things and the way the other person does things. That does not necessarily mean that the other persons way of doing something is bad practice. Don't just challenge because someone does things differently to you.

- *Opinions*
There will be differences between what you think and what the person you are challenging thinks.

If you bear all of the above in mind, when deciding *how* to challenge, your approach is much more likely to be effective. In addition, we believe that it is important to choose the least oppressive way of challenging someone.

When should you challenge?
This is very closely linked to thinking around the area of *how* to challenge. Is it appropriate to challenge at the time or later?

Consequences of challenging
In addition to considering the questions we have outlined, it is also important to think about the consequences of any challenge both in terms of yourself and the person you are challenging. You should also think about the needs of the 'victim' of the oppression/oppressive practice. Do you need to locate support systems? etc.

When Jane is visiting Mr Hamlin, he tells her "the area has really gone downhill since all the Blacks moved in." Jane recognises this as an overtly racist comment and wants to challenge it. She says "I wouldn't agree with you on that Mr Hamlin. It sounds like a sweeping statement to me and is very unfair to Black people." She then reports the comment to her manager and makes a record of what Mr Hamlin said and how she responded. In her next supervision session, she discusses the incident and says she would have handled it quite differently had a staff member made the comment. She tells her manager she would have been more assertive in disagreeing and would have used the word racism and referred to agency policies and procedures.

SECTION TWO: HUMAN DEVELOPMENT

This section covers some of the theories about how people develop –
beginning with child development and moving on through a whole life.
Most human development theories are drawn from psychology and
there are many different theories. This section explores just a few of
these.

Reading this section you will learn more about:

- Child development models
- Erikson's eight stages of man
- Piaget's child development stages
- Vygotsky's writing
- The nature/nurture debate
- Adult development models
- Maslow's hierarchy of needs
- Attachment theory
- Identity
- Self image
- Self esteem
- Biographical approach
- Life story work
- Reminiscence work

CHILD DEVELOPMENT

There are various theories and models of child development. Some of these focus on the child's intellectual development (eg. Piaget), others seek to embrace the social and emotional development of a child (eg. Erikson).

Most of the models have one thing in common. They consider that there are definable stages that the vast majority of children go through. These stages are driven by the biological and physical development of the child.

This means that children go through "developmental milestones" (each child should be able to do a certain thing eg. walk by a certain age, about 18 months).

Developmental milestones should not be used too rigidly since children can develop at different rates. However, if a child is late in attaining (or does not reach) a number of developmental milestones, then it is a sign that they may benefit from additional support.

ERIKSON

Erik Erikson (1950) developed a model of human development titled the "Eight Ages of Man". Erikson described each stage as a struggle between two emotional opposites. The first stage is characterised by the emotions trust and mistrust. The child's experience would result in the child adopting one of these emotions as a dominant (unconscious) outlook. If the child came through the first stage trusting people, there is still a chance that future negative experiences could result in the child losing trust in those around them.

The five stages that relate to children are:

Stage One: Trust-mistrust. Age 0 to 1 year. The child will feel able to trust the world and people in the world if their needs are responded to and the child is cared for. Emotional warmth and a sense of belonging from adult caregivers are crucial to building up a sense of trust.

Inadequate and rejecting care from adults will result in the child being suspicious and fearful of adults and others.

Stage Two: Antonomy – Doubt. Age 1 to 3 years. Erikson argues that this was the first opportunity the child has to develop a range of life skills. Encouraging this is key to building up the child's confidence. If the child is not positively supported to develop their own skills, or is mocked or criticised when they do learn new skills then the child will be riddled with doubt and lack confidence.

Stage Three: Initiative – Inadequacy (or guilt). Age 3 to 6 years. The child has already got control over their body and their life skills are being increased. In stage three, the child feels able to initiate actions, both physical and verbal. Children who are supported to initiate physical activities, such a bike riding, swimming etc will have their sense of initiative reinforced. Emotional and intellectual initiative will be reinforced by the child's questions being answered whilst conversation and play are encouraged.

If the child's initiative is not encouraged the child will develop a sense of guilt or inadequacy over self initiated activities.

Stage Four: Industry – Inferiority. Age 6 to 12 years. The child has a strong interest in matters of detail. How things work, why events happen, how things are made are all key questions and points of interest for the child.

Children will need to be encouraged in their activities of making, sewing and baking. The end products need to be praised. It is in this sense that the child is industrious. However, if the child's making activities are dismissed as "making a mess" then this can instil a sense of inferiority in the child.

This is also the first stage where the child is aware of other children. The child's sense of industry or inferiority can be shaped by their relative achievements in respect of their peers.

Stage Five: Identity – Role Confusion. Age 12 to 18 years. The child is developing into an adolescent. There are significant biological changes resulting in new feelings and sensations. The adolescent is also increasingly aware of the importance of what other people may think of them. Intellectually, the adolescent is also able to generate ideal images (of family, friendships and society) and contrast them with the imperfections they experience on a daily basis.

Erikson highlighted the importance of identity formation. For the adolescent this is drawn from their family, their own interests and activities, their peers and their aspirations for the future. If the adolescent has had positive experiences in the first four stages of their life, this should result in a higher probability that they will develop a positive identity.

However, such a positive outcome is not guaranteed and a variety of factors could result in the adolescent experiencing role confusion. It was Erikson who introduced the term identity crisis. This role confusion or identity crisis could be generated by:

- the adolescent being unfavourably compared to others
- the adolescent having an interest that their family look down on
- societal expectations eg. young women are slim, young men will earn lots of money etc and the young person does not 'fit in'.

For some young people, a negative identity is applied to them by others (parents or teachers etc). There is a risk that this informal labelling will result in a self fulfilling prophecy (the adolescent who is labelled 'lazy' by a teacher then does not do their work etc).

PIAGET

Jean Piaget developed his stage theory of intellectual development from the 1920s onwards. (For example Piaget, 1928.)

Piaget identified four stages. A child moves from one stage to the next as a result of various factors that aid development. These factors are:

- Maturation; this is the physical and cognitive growth that occurs as the child grows up.
- Experience; this is acquired by the child as they engage with the physical world around them.
- Social interaction; the child engages with other people. Piaget was particularly aware of the influences of other (often older) children.
- Equilibration is the way the child draws the first three factors together to establish logic and consistency.

The four stages of development Piaget identified are:

- First stage: Sensorimotor stage. Aged 0 to 2 years. The child uses their senses to actively explore their world. The child becomes aware of their separateness from the world around them. Towards the end of this stage, the child is starting to experiment with objects to see how they fall or move etc.

- Second stage: Preoperational stage. Aged 2 to 6 years. During this stage, the child is egocentric. They are very focussed on their own perspective. Early on in this stage when children play together, it can be as if the children each play their own game, even though they could be side by side.

  The child has a view of the world that is objective. Rules are absolute. During this stage, the child grasps the difference in gender and gender roles.

- Third stage: Concrete operational. Aged 7 to 12 years. The child begins to develop their own logic and can organise thoughts in a consistent framework.

  Abstract reasoning is still too difficult but physical objects and mathematical problems can be worked on (adding, subtracting and multiplication etc).

  Egocentric outlook comes to an end in Stage 3.

- Fourth stage: Formal operations. Aged 11 to 15 years. The young person is able to grasp hypothetical ideas and abstract thinking. The young person can test out theories or hypotheses. Abstract thinking can extend to algebraic mathematics. This stage continues into adulthood.

VYGOTSKY

In contrast to Piaget's account of cognitive development Lev Vygotsky (1934) wrote about child and adult development in the 1930s that focussed on the impact of culture and society. Vygotsky argued that biological development was significant until the age of 2 or so. After that, although biological development continued this was secondary to the impact of culture, which Vygotsky claims is far more significant. As an illustration Vygotsky points out that biologically speaking humans across the world are very similar. However, there is a huge diversity in how people live and this cannot be explained in terms of biology. It is culture that has generated and then sustains this diversity.

Another of Vygotsky's points is that so much human development is shaped by language (eg. memory, emotions, reasoning, personality, relationships etc). All language is socially constructed.

Vygotsky's approach is very developed and is difficult to condense. His key point (the importance of culture in generating and shaping child development) is worth hanging on to.

NATURE/NURTURE DEBATE

The perspectives on child development which we have outlined are also key aspects of the nature/nurture debate. The main outline of each camp is:

Nature: Human development is largely a biological process that occurs automatically and follows common (shared) stages.

Much of our character, intelligence and our physique/looks is determined by our genes. We will be the way we will be! Nothing can change this.

Nurture: At first, biological development is significant. However, by the time the child is about one, then social relationships and cultural customs will start to profoundly influence the child's personality. Intelligence is not set, it will be markedly enhanced by a stimulating environment (or stunted by a barren care environment).

Sexuality and gender are also not biologically rigid. Gender roles are culturally decided (eg. men work in heavy industry, women look after the family home). Even sexual orientation is malleable. In ancient Greece, among the aristocracy and in the army, male homosexuality was the preferred sexual orientation. Aristocratic men in Greece married women to continue the family line.

Both sides in the nature/nurture debate look at families where behaviour patterns are repeated by one generation to the next. Where a parent develops mental health problems and then a son or daughter develops mental health problems, is this a sign of genetics or is the son or daughter (unconsciously) modelling the behaviour of their parents? The son or daughter has a 'green light' to exhibit the same type of behaviours their parents have.

ADULT DEVELOPMENT

Adult development is a general term that recognises that most adults go through various changes in their life. Each change presents the person with opportunities and potential problems. How the person adjusts to the changes is influenced by how significant any change is, the person's personality and character, their support networks and resources and so on.

Adult development has increasingly emphasised the diversity that exists and that we must not assume that all individuals will progress along one set route.

Child development is characterised by identifiable stages that the vast majority of children will progress through. This includes biological development (their bodies) as well as educational development or development of intelligence, language, moral development etc.

When it comes to adult development, there is less agreement as to whether it is helpful to talk of stages.

Erik Erikson (1950) argued that there are identifiable stages. Erikson stated there are Eight Ages of human development. Five of these related to children, three to adults.

Erikson claimed that each stage was a struggle between two competing emotional and personality based characteristics. The first five stages are reviewed in the section on child development. The three stages that relate to adults are:

- Stage Six; Intimacy versus isolation. The person is aged 18 to about 40. In this stage, the adult seeks to establish close meaningful relationships. The relationships do not have to be sexual at all; the important aspect is that there is a mutual emotional bond. If the adult does not establish relationships that have this closeness, the person will have a sense of isolation.
- Stage Seven; Generativity versus self absorption. Middle age. In this stage the person will show an interest in the world beyond their immediate family. They will be motivated by a concern for

society, the environment and future generations. If a person does not cultivate this outlook, they will become self absorbed and primarily concerned for their own material or hedonistic pursuits.

- Stage Eight: Integrity versus despair. The person is aged about 60 years old or more. The person has time for reflection and as they look back on their life, they may have a sense of satisfaction; this will lead to a feeling of integrity. If the person's reflection results in them feeling they missed key opportunities, then there is an increased risk of experiencing despair. This is partly generated by the sense that it is too late to change anything.

Other writers on adult development are not so committed to the stages model. Even Erikson recognised that the Generativity stage was not tied to middle aged people. Teenagers can show a concern for the world, it's not just middle aged people who want to save the planet!

Hence, many writers on adult development do not promote a stages model. Whilst writers recognise that biological changes do occur (especially the menopause and the process of ageing), many writers argue that outside of these biological changes there is no clear human development.

For adults, biological changes are just one factor shaping their life. There are lots of other factors or influences that can have a greater effect on them. Adults do not go through similar emotional and psychological stages at the same time or at similar rates. Some people become wiser as they grow older, some people don't. Physically, one of the main age related factors is the decline in vision, hearing and information processing as we get older.

There does appear to be a history or generational effect on human development. The people who lived through the Second World War may have a different view to consumption, spending and waste compared to people who have lived through the 1990's. Even if there are generational effects, it still needs to be noted that there are differences within a generation (not all people who were young adults in the 1990's spend and throw away).

Human development models have also emphasised that for any one individual, change is unique to that person and occurs due to random social and environmental events. Some of these events are relatively common but others aren't. Examples include the effect that the following have on a person:

- relationships and breakdown of relationships
- having a serious illness or acquiring a disability
- being a victim of crime
- business failure (or success)
- significant promotion (or being made redundant)
- death of a close family member

There can be other unique events. Some individuals meet a charismatic person and so they embark on a totally new life direction (be it lifestyle, work, spirituality etc).

In human development circles the randomness of life changing events has generated discussion about how much choice and control we actually have in our lives.

Hence, adult development models have identified three general influences on adulthood:

- There are some biological age related factors but these are mainly confined to changes that occur later in life.
- There do appear to be generational factors as a result of societal pressures or opportunities.
- The main influences in any one person's life are quite random but they can have a profound impact on a person's life direction.

MASLOW'S HIERARCHY OF NEEDS

Maslow (1970) argues that all humans have a hierarchy of needs. We first need to satisfy basic biological needs (eg food, warmth etc) and then we are successively drawn to meet higher needs.

Originally Maslow created a pyramid of needs with five levels. He later extended this to seven levels.

The Pyramid of Needs

Aesthetic Needs Some people have a need to see or experience beauty, symmetry in art, environment, music etc

To Know and Understand We have a need to know, to understand and to explain.

Self Actualisation Need Need for self fulfilment to reach our potential.

Esteem Needs To have self respect, self esteem and to have esteem from others.

Belongingness and Love Needs To give and receive love, to belong in a family, group, clan or nation.

Safety and Security Needs Physical safety but also law and order, social stability, continuity, job security etc.

Physiological (or Biological) Needs such as the need for food, warmth, drink, sleep.

The Strength of the Needs

Maslow argued that each level of need was a very powerful motivating force for each person.

At first, we are preoccupied with meeting our physiological (or biological) needs. If our need for food, water, warmth etc is not being met, then all the other 'higher' needs are unimportant. We must satisfy our biological needs. Once we are in a situation where our biological needs are largely or fully met, we start to experience a craving for safety and security. The more fully our biological needs are met, the stronger is our desire to establish safety and security. The safety and security needs are not just about being free of the fear of being physically attacked. It also refers to our need for stability, order and routine. This includes social and economic stability.

Once the safety and security needs are largely or fully met, then our need for belonging and love becomes as intense as the two preceding needs once were. We crave the opportunity to love and to be loved, to belong to someone else, to be part of a wider group or community.

When we satisfy or largely meet our need to love and be loved, the importance of our need for self esteem starts to rise in importance. This need includes being able to achieve tasks, being competent, independent and having personal strength. Additionally, we need respect from others in the form of prestige, status – even fame. Maslow noted that just basing self esteem on the opinion of others was inviting insecurity. We need a sense that self esteem is based on deserved respect from others rather than celebrity or unwarranted adulation.

The need for self actualisation increases as our need for esteem is satisfied. Maslow assumes that all people will experience this need. How this need is satisfied will be an expression of our individuality. For one person, it will be through being an ideal mother; for another person, achieving a physical, athletic goal; for yet a different person, developing a new invention etc.

In his later writings, Maslow then added on two higher stages. In some respects they are extensions of the self actualisation stage rather than entirely new stages.

In the first of the two new stages (the sixth stage of the whole pyramid) Maslow argued that we have a need to know, to be curious to seek to understand our world. People who enter into boring, unstimulating lifestyles are at risk of developing mental health problems.

The second of the two new stages (the seventh stage of the whole pyramid) is the aesthetic need. Maslow recognised that this need may only be felt by some people. However, for these people the need to experience beauty, symmetry and idealised harmony was so strong that Maslow felt it should be considered a need.

Maslow made clear that people did not need to work through the stages in a methodical, rigid manner. A person could be seeking to meet their needs from two or three stages at the same time. But a person would only be able to increasingly devote their personal resources to a higher stage once a lower stage was largely satisfied.

Perspectives on Maslow's Hierarchy of Needs

Maslow's Hierarchy of Needs has been a very significant standard in seeking to explain human motivation and the human condition. It is incredibly popular.

Within psychology, it has been difficult to generate research that can adequately test the theory. Some psychologists like the theory so much they have developed it further, either by increasing or reducing the number of stages. Other psychologists have pointed out its weakness and the way there are individuals who do not follow the staged progression.

Maslow's Hierarchy of Needs and Care Services

Potentially, Maslow's theory could be a very helpful measure for services that are seeking to develop person centred care. The pyramid provides staff with clearly identifiable stages that they could support service users to progress through.

The pyramid could also be used to evaluate (even if only in broad measure) the quality of service provision.

Worryingly there are too many services that only support service users as far as level two. Some services don't even get as high as level two (safety and security). There are service users who fear arbitrary decisions from domineering and volatile staff; there are service users who are anxious over the next push, hit or scream from another service user.

Very few service users are actively supported to have their needs around love and belonging met. Additionally, the use of labels in services cuts across upholding a persons self esteem and their sense that others respect them as competent people.

Staff can use the hierarchy of needs positively as a guide to developing person centred, holistic care. How can a service support each service user to work through the levels and achieve their own goals as fully as possible?

ATTACHMENT THEORY AND CHILDREN

The main point of attachment theory is that all children are born with an innate need to feel loved and wanted by their parents. If a child does not feel this, the child has a sense of emotional hurt that results in the child engaging in a range of behaviours that are intended to get the parent to love the child, but often the behaviours appear counter productive.

One of the fundamental needs of children to ensure optimal emotional and behavioural development, are secure attachments to the child's parents (or significant adult caregivers) from the beginning of the child's life.

Attachment theory was first promoted by Bowlby (1969, 1973, 1980). Since Bowlby first wrote about attachment many other writers have added to our knowledge. Examples include Ainsworth et al (1978); Rutter (1995), Belsky and Cassidy (1994). There are many more writers. The main impression to convey is that attachment theory is considered proved beyond reasonable doubt.

Every child has an innate need to feel loved and wanted by their parents. It is a parental responsibility to meet this need. Where attachments to parents are broken the child needs to have secure attachments established with alternative adult caregivers, ideally, before the child is aged 3, or as soon as possible after the attachment to the parent is ruptured.

Where a child has parents who do not make the child feel secure or where attachments have been ruptured there is a significant risk of the child having difficulty with a range of relationships and their problem solving and coping skills can be poorer. There is also a risk of the person, when they are adults (and parents), failing to provide secure attachments to their own children (and so the cycle continues).

The evidence around the effect of secure and insecure attachments is clear.

Secure attachments

- Promote security
- Enhance a child's development of independence skills
- Foster a child's ability to establish social relationships
- Enables a child to explore and investigate the wider world
- Facilitates play

Whilst it may sound strange, one of the ways that children develop and mature is through play.

Attachment theory makes clear that when a child senses that their attachments to their adult caregivers are not secure then they focus their emotions and behaviours on trying to re-establish their attachment (attachment behaviours are activated).

The child cannot engage in play and exploration when attachment behaviours are activated. The child's play shuts down (in terms of continuing to aid development).

The effect of this is clear. It is not unusual for a support worker or foster carer to notice that, say, a child aged 10 plays best with a 7 year old. Sometimes the foster carer or staff member may say the child appears immature for a 10 year old. This could be because the child has attachment anxieties.

Since the child is a child (obviously) then they do not have the language and emotional development of an adult. Therefore when attachment anxieties are triggered the child is not able to verbally express themselves. They express their attachment anxiety through their behaviours (attachment behaviours).

Attachment theory has established that there are three insecure types of attachment, each of which generates certain responses in the child (Howe et al, 2000).

1.   Avoidant/Defended Attachment Anxiety

- Child rejected, may just be emotional rejection but may include physical violence
- Child downplays attachment

- Child minimises expressions of distress, the child knows that when their parent is shouting at them if the child is distressed this results in further parental rejection
- Child acts happy even when frightened
- Child shows aggression when they are dominant, e.g. at school with weaker children or with younger brother or sister

2.   Ambivalent/Coercive Attachment Anxiety

- Unpredictable/insensitive care giving. Often characterised by neglect or disinterest in child. But there are times when child feels cared for and loved
- Child maximises expression of distress, especially when parent about to leave
- Child engages in attention seeking behaviour this can include the child ignoring the parent when back together, the child is communicating (but not saying verbally) "show me you love me"
- Child desires close relationships but is anxious over risk of withdrawal of affection, this can include child hanging around the parent for long periods of time

3.   Disorganised/Controlling Attachment Anxiety

- A child finds this type of parenting the most difficult to adapt to
- Care givers are unpredictable and rejecting – this may just be emotional rejection but can include violence
- Care giver is frightening or frightened – a source of distress for the child. The care giver (parent) may have a drug or alcohol dependency or mental health problems. This effects the care giver's personality which causes the child distress
- If the child gets closer to care giver the child gets more distressed since the child becomes more aware of the impact of the parent's drug or alcohol dependency etc
- Child feels they are unloved and the child feels they are the cause of others anger
- Child flooded with emotions of fear and anger
- Child has fear of being in danger and feeling out of control, the child's behaviours can be inconsistent and destructive
- Only predictable aspect is the child, therefore they try to control themselves
- Child develops defences and inhibitions to maintain control

- Child can see themselves as strong, powerful but also bad. View of child as bad is impressed on child by parent who labels child as a bad child
- Child can stop fearing danger
- Child fears losing control – fears their feelings may overwhelm them. Child gives impression of being strong, assertive, even arrogant. This is a heavily defended façade. Behind the façade is emotional turmoil.

Attachment theory is often characterised as claiming that the first five years of a child's life are crucial in terms of establishing secure attachments. We would argue that attachment applies throughout a child and young person's life. Indeed there is increasing interest in the way attachments effect adult behaviour (see following section).

Foster carers and workers need to be aware that attachment behaviours change as the child becomes a young person, but the reason and intention behind them remain the same.

A teenager who is experiencing ambivalent/ coercive attachment anxiety is also likely to engage in attention seeking behaviour. Unlike a seven year old, who may lie on the floor kicking and crying, a teenager may engage in self-harm, sexual activity or consume alcohol and then make sure that their parent is aware.

Attachment and Anti-Oppressive Practice

Within residential care settings children and young people will need the opportunity to form selective attachments. Unfortunately these are always at risk of being ruptured and the young people will find the separation from important attachments stressful. Such separation is nearly always against the child's wishes (e.g. worker moves to new job).

It is clear that children can cope with several adults looking after them. In some cultures this is the norm with aunts, grandparents and parents all involved in the care of a child or children. However, children need to have the same group of adults look after them over time. Additionally it is best if the child can go to the principle care givers at times when the child is tired, distressed or facing challenging circumstances.

Care services that have more stable staff teams with little turnover are likely to provide children and young people with a more secure environment.

In more day to day matters behaviours by staff that reinforce attachment and reduce experiences of rejection can help children feel secure. Staff need to consider how they express views on finishing shifts and going on annual leave. Do staff say "I can't wait for 3 o'clock!" (when they finish work).

On a broader level is the question of "can services make a determined attempt to reduce placement moves?"

A child who is in foster care or in a care home may have a settled period when they first arrive and it may be a very positive experience. Then the child may start to engage in behaviours that threaten the placement.

The child may be doing this because they have learnt that adult care givers cannot be trusted. The experience of previous rejection is so painful for the child that they seek to protect themselves by rejecting the new adult care givers before they (the child) are rejected again!

One approach is to try to express to the child what they may be (unconsciously) thinking. "You're doing this because you want to control me,"; "You think I'm going to reject you..." etc. The child, in any verbal response, is likely to dismiss what you say. You will tell if you are on the right lines by non-verbal responses, facial expressions or if their behaviour calms down (at least temporarily).

Olliver-Kneafsey (2003) says that being unpredictable with the child can be useful. The child with attachment anxiety thinks consistency and reliability won't last so seeks to disrupt first.

Olliver-Kneafsey (2003) also suggest that conveying to the child that they have a choice is important "You are choosing to ignore me today", "You are choosing not to get dressed" etc. Any changes in the child's behaviour will not occur quickly. Two to five years is probably a realistic time frame. With each placement move the clock gets put back to zero.

Even if a child remains in a placement they can have unsettled periods. Contact with a birth parent who may say "I love you" can leave the child struggling. The child cannot reconcile their parents spoken words with their situation (continued separation). Additionally for many looked after children they are aware that their parent is still caring for a sibling or half brother/sister or step brother/sister. This leaves the child with the painful, unanswered question "Why love them but not me?"

Olliver-Kneafsey (2003) comments that time, a positive mental attitude and a calm objective approach are all good investments with a child with attachment issues. The child's (unconscious) anger, hurt and turmoil will mean that they try to generate anger in the adults around them. The adult caregivers need to try to avoid getting drawn into angry conflicts with the child. Again, as a response, express, as a best guess, why you think the child is doing what they are doing, or just suggest to the child that they are finding their situation difficult at the moment.

A family support worker is asked to support a family. The 14 year old teenager, Amber, is refusing to attend school. Her older sister, Amy, aged 16 does attend school. The support worker quickly senses that Amy is mother's favourite daughter. A 12 year old brother lives with their father. Their father is now in a new relationship and lives 5 miles away.

The mother had a partner who was so violent the mother attempted suicide. The mother is now a lone parent. Conflict between Amber and her mother has been rising. At one point Amber's mother threatened to kill herself due to how stressful she is finding the arguments with Amber. Following this, Amber stopped attending school.

The support worker had a good idea why Amber was refusing to attend school. The son is loved by dad, Amy by mother but Amber is left asking, "Who loves me?" Amber loves her mother but the mother's threat to kill herself has triggered significant attachment anxiety in Amber, so she wants to stay close to her mother in case she tries to kill herself.

The support worker realises she can't 'lecture' the family about their situation. Through planned activities, the support worker enables Amber to express her concerns. As a result Amber's mother admits she should not have threatened to kill herself. She also agrees to spend time with Amber. Amber starts to attend school again.

ATTACHMENT THEORY AND ADULTS

Attachment theory as it applies to adults recognises that most adults have a basic need to feel loved and wanted by another adult. If an adult experiences rejection this can have an adverse effect on their ability to form and develop other relationships.

Originally, attachment theory was developed from studying the relationships children had with their parents. In the last 15 years or so there has been increasing interest in the application of attachment theory to adults.

Attachment theory can apply to adults in the following ways:

1. If an adult grew up feeling that they were not loved and wanted by one or both of their parents, then this could have a continuing impact on their ability to form stable relationships both with other adults and with any children they then have.

    It is difficult to predict exactly how an adult will respond. An adult who felt unloved as a child may, when they develop a romantic relationship, become completely dependent on that other adult. In many ways, this is fine so long as the relationship is long lasting. Another adult with a similar childhood experience may initially establish an intensive romantic relationship but then break it abruptly.

    The main 'escape' for an adult is that they become aware of how their childhood experiences are affecting their relationship with other adults. They will need to become conscious of the sense of insecurity they have and why they behave in the way they do in their relationships with other adults (or their own children).

An adult needs to become conscious of their own insecurities. Then when they are in a situation in which their anxieties are triggered instead of responding unconsciously (eg. promising never ending love or breaking the relationship entirely) they should be able to have some sense of choice as to how to respond. One response may be to discuss with their partner why they are experiencing the emotions they are presently feeling and what they would 'instinctively' do in response. The hope is that by being conscious and by being able to express themselves, whilst the adult may still feel insecure they can engage in behaviours that are less extreme and more controlled. In this way they are able to prevent situations occurring that appear to repeat previous situations in their life.

2.   An adult may experience rejection due to some aspect that is part of them but which is devalued by society. Obvious examples are physical disability, learning disability or mental health problems.

The person with the disability or mental health problem may (and probably did) experience rejection as a child. They may not have been rejected by their parents (who may have been loving and caring) but the person may have experienced rejection either from individuals or through being treated differently such as by being sent to a special school.

If the person had a positive childhood, there is still a risk that they will experience rejection and exclusion as an adult because they are seen as different (and not as good as others). They could then start to engage in behaviours that are an expression of their attachment anxieties. Due to a fear of future rejection the person may show little or no interest in developing new relationships or going to new groups or organisations. The adult may say they are lonely and have no friends but the fear of rejection may leave them socially paralysed. Unfortunately care staff can then label the person as lacking in self motivation or not taking responsibility for their own development etc.

If the adult is in a care service, the experience of the care service can compound and increase an adult's attachment anxiety. Comments by staff (I'm on annual leave next week – yippee), staff behaviours at work (clustering with other staff in an office, behind a closed door) and just the regular turnover of staff leaving, can all heighten a person's sense that they are still not loved and wanted for the person they are.

Sometimes when a new member of staff starts at a service, staff comment that a particular service user "tries it on" with the new staff member. Sometimes a service user may be aggressive to a new staff member. It could be argued that the service user is asking "Can I trust you?" Often the service user cannot sustain such a position (testing out the staff member) due to their own needs for support. Too often, however, the service user will find that they are let down by individual staff or the service.

An older person who has been cared for by a family member (partner, son or daughter) and has now had to enter a care home (against the service user's true wishes) could display attachment behaviours towards that family member when they are visited by the family member. Like so many attachment behaviours they appear counter productive. The older person in care may ignore their visitor, or they may be angry towards them. Rationally speaking the service user should convey to the family member how important their relationship is to them and how hurt they feel now they are in a care service. But such a rational perspective is the luxury of those who are not emotionally involved in a key relationship that always carried with it a sense of being loved, wanted and needed.

IDENTITY

Some identity issues have already been covered in this section. However, identity is such an important factor in working with people that it is worth taking a more detailed look at ideas about identity in terms of both children and adults. Of course it is important for staff who work with adults to understand identity in children, as adults have all been children once and if adults are to have a positive sense of their identity then this needs to begin in childhood.

Identity is partly an expression of two cognitive functions – self image and self esteem:

- Self image is essentially about how we see or describe ourselves
- Self esteem is about how we value ourselves

　　　　　　　copyright© Kirwin Maclean Associates

IDENTITY ISSUES IN CHILDHOOD

Central to identity formation is the child's sense of self. Children's sense of self includes aspects like:

- Name
- Family, the type of relationship with family and identification with family members
- Culture
- Activities and interests engaged in
- Gender
- Religion
- Race and Ethnicity

The list could go on.

The Development of Identity

Argyle (1969) has related that there are four stages to identity development:

1. When children are very young their parents are the most significant people in the child's life. The young child incorporates into their personality the perception, attitudes and reactions of the parent. This includes the parents reactions to the child themselves.
2. It's not long before the young child starts to compare themselves to others. Certain aspects of self image only develop through comparison (e.g. height, speed at running and other skills).
3. As the child grows up social roles become more important. Within the family the child already has a role (son/daughter, brother, sister). This may be added to by place in the family. Further roles and responsibilities develop as schooling starts and when interests and activities are pursued.
4. As the child grows older identification occurs. The child looks to role models who they can identify with. Classically this occurs in adolescence but the process starts before the person is a teenager.

Self-Esteem and Confidence

At the same time as building up their sense of identity the child needs to feel that their identity is positive and they can value themselves as they are.

Most children will start this process within their family where they experience being loved by parents and other family members. Family members will talk about the things they like about the child. Self-esteem and confidence will be enhanced by family members encouraging the child to extend their skills. As with all successful skill development the skill to be learned should be at the top end of what the child can achieve. When the child successfully learns the new skills, and is praised, the child's confidence is enhanced. They will then be willing to continue to try to learn new skills.

Skill acquisition should be across a broad range of activities. By being involved in different activities the child's sense of identity is broadened. If the child's development in one area is limited then this should not overwhelm the child since there will be another area in which they are acquiring new skills.

Individuality and Group Identity

Young people with positive identity development will be able to:

1. See themselves as an individual, distinct from others
2. See themselves as one of a group, joining with other individuals who have shared characteristics. The person is likely to associate with several groups e.g. family; sport or interest group; cultural/community group etc. The person should take pride in group identity

Biographical Approach

Self image or how we describe ourselves can also be described as how we understand our own biography.

> "A stable self identity is based on an account of a person's life, actions and influences which make sense to themselves and which can be explained to other people without difficulty."

Giddens (1991)

Within this definition of identity are at least two aspects that looked after children can struggle with.

- A life which makes sense to themselves. For some looked after children their life doesn't make sense to themselves. Separation from parents and being cared for by other adults may be difficult to understand. Services often respond to this by supporting young people write life stories.
- An account which can be explained to other people without difficulty. Many looked after children feel they cannot tell friends much about themselves. Ryan and Walker (1999) recommend that foster carers and staff should support the young people they work with develop a 'cover story'. There should be no lies or fabrications in a cover story. In their cover story the child may be selective about their life but their cover story is true and enables the child to give a socially acceptable and logical explanation for who they are and why they are there. If a child does not have a cover story then they are at risk of lying to people they meet. If the fabrications are exposed the child is quickly given a negative label.

Children's Services and Identity

Children in contact with services and especially looked after children are at risk of having difficulties with their sense of identity and of having poor self esteem.

Foster carers and staff in children's services therefore need to work with children to enhance their sense of self and self esteem. Aspects of the type of work possible have already been referred to.

- Life story work. This is a focussed activity, usually done on a one to one basis, where a worker supports a service user to discuss their life and all the changes that have occurred.

    A life story book is usually generated so that the knowledge can be preserved and the life story book becomes the property of the service user.

    Life story work has been particularly useful with looked after children and children with a learning disability. It can support the service user gain a clearer understanding of the changes that have occurred and why they have occurred.

- Books and other resources. Related to life story work are the number of books and other resources that can support children with identity issues recognise that there are many other children who have experienced similar life events.

- Service user forums and meetings. Bringing together looked after children and young people can be a very empowering experience. Probably most successful in the 15-18 age group (as young people prepare to leave care), but it can also be useful for younger age groups.

- Encouraging a range of interests and activities. This enables children and young people to have a sense of what they like and who they are, in a positive sense.

- Where appropriate, maximising contact with birth family. Identity and family are inextricably linked.

- Mentoring. When a young person is paired with a mentor this can enable the young person to have a positive sense of their own identity.

Charlotte and Alan are foster carers. Whenever a child is placed with them, they develop a "memory book" with the child which includes photos of themselves, their house and the family pets. They see this as an important contribution to helping children understand their experiences. The memory books are often used by the children's social workers as part of a life story approach.

Identity and Children from Black and Minority Ethnic Communities

Children from black and minority ethnic communities who are in contact with children's services are likely to have additional needs due to their experience of racism and discrimination within a white society.

The shortage of foster placements has resulted in looked after Black children being placed with white foster carers. Wherever possible Black children should be placed with foster carers who have the same racial and cultural identity as the child. For the Black child the importance of this cannot be exaggerated in terms of positive identity development and learning the skills to counter racism and discrimination.

Dutt and Phillips (2000) have highlighted how services need to support the Black child to:

- Develop their awareness of their own ethnicity in terms of personal, family and community history. Where the information is not already available then services should obtain it.
- Enjoy lived experiences of their culture such as attendance at celebrations or festivals which include music, food and traditional rituals.
- Be brought up in their family belief systems – religion, rights and traditions.
- Have the opportunity to learn about and maintain family languages.

Sue and Simon are foster carers. They have two young childen placed with them who are Jewish. Recognising the need to promote the children's identity Sue and Simon make links with a local synagogue to find out about festivals and customs. They are invited to bring the children along to a weekly children's group meeting. Sue and Simon talk through the available opportunities with the children's social worker pointing out what support they need to promote the children's identity.

IDENTITY ISSUES FOR ADULTS

The importance of having a unique identity and positive sense of self (good self esteem) are just as important for adults as for children.

In respect of adults who have contact with social care services there are various threats to their positive sense of identity and self esteem.

1.   *Societal Prejudice and Discrimination*

In the section on oppression, we discussed how there can be oppression at a societal level. Many adults in society are aware of

---

the way they are discriminated against and this can have an effect on self confidence and generate a range of responses (including defensiveness, anger or mental health issues). The person may, or may not, have social care needs. One of the main counters to society negatively valuing people of a certain identity is for individuals to join together either just for mutual support and have a positive sense of identity or to campaign for equality (eg: gay men).

2.   *Institutional Stigma*

Being in contact with social care services can still carry a stigma. This is partly because in the past the quality of social care services for adults was poor. Even today there are examples where service provision can be very poor (eg. Healthcare Commission report on services to adults with learning disabilities by Cornwall Partnership Trust 2006). Even disregarding these high profile cases, there are still too many residential care homes where even a short visit tells you "I wouldn't like to live here!". There are still care homes where you walk in and smell urine; there are homes where the office phone rings throughout the building (and still appears to be unanswered); there are homes where the environment is noisy and unsettling or service users have no contact with staff outside of personal care; there can be an air of stale boredom or waiting for death.

This is added to by the active support a service provides. Does the service assist adults to go to a 'disco' that is from 7.00pm to 9.00pm where only soft drinks are sold or does the service assist the service user to go to a summer rock festival for a weekend?

Therefore the image a service creates in the minds of others could influence how people view service users. However the service user may have a history and identity that is quite different from the image that the service projects.

3.   *Individual Attitudes*

The attitudes and behaviour of staff can be a key element of supporting adult service users maintain (or develop) their identity and self esteem.

Many staff receive a copy of the poem "Look Closer; See Me" (the account by an older woman who looks back over her life) early on in their training. That poem symbolises how staff can unconsciously apply generalised labels (eg. older person) onto a person that covers their identity like a blanket and in the eyes of staff gives the person an identity that is for staff convenience. Other examples include:

- Any of the 'ic' phrases eg. "schizophrenic," "alcoholic", "diabetic" etc
- Challenging behaviour, "She's a hair puller" etc
- Misusing a person's condition eg "He's a Downs"
- Even informal comments like "He is an attention seeker" "She is a real manipulator" etc

Blanket labels like this do a great disservice to service users. People have likes and dislikes, culture and language, family and friends, loves and passions, beliefs and values etc. These need to be recognised and celebrated by staff and services. It is important for staff to challenge negative attitudes and to promote a positive sense of identity for service users.

Promoting Identity

Many services have made progress in recognising and respecting the identity of service users.

At an institutional level, the development of person centred plans and person centred care is one way in which services are trying to acknowledge a person's identity and work from there.

In respect of services that work with adults of working age, many services are seeking to give more relevant options. These options include further education, training for employment and support to get a job. Day time occupation is a key aspect of identity. Often if you meet someone new the first question is "What is your name?" the second question "What do you do?"

Meaningful day occupation is also a key aspect of self esteem. Where a service user is unlikely to get a job then many services still support the service user to contribute, in some way, to their community. Many services assist service users to raise money for a charity or campaign for a local cause, this can have a direct effect on positive feelings of self esteem.

Services are also developing a more positive approach to risk assessment and risk management. Often the key decisions around risk management are made in multi-disciplinary meetings but the view of the service user is now taken far more seriously. If services respect the service users wishes, then often the service user can still live their life as they want to even if there is risk involved.

Personal relationships are a significant aspect of identity. This is partly because our sexuality is a key part of who we are. Some services have developed a more positive attitude to this but there are still other services where managers either overlook or ignore or are paralysed by the thought of supporting service users in this area.

Many service users who are single want a partner. Even services that want to support the service user can find this difficult (they can't conjure up true love or even a hot date). But services do assist the service user by ensuring that planned social activities (where the service user could meet someone) do occur and the service user is supported to develop relationships without unjustified and intrusive interference (eg. bedroom doors propped open, or ten minute checks "Are you both alright in there?" – even the staff member asking that knows what the answer is!)

There have been interesting service developments in this area including the establishment of dating agencies and individual support plans that recognise individual's sexuality.

Services can also support adults in terms of affirming their own identity directly. This can be in the form of life story work, reminiscence or even genealogy.

In life story work with adults with a learning disability, the aim is to generate a book or a personal record (DVD?) of that person's life. It becomes their property. Where a person has experienced many changes it can result in them understanding more about their life.

Life story work activities can include visiting former placements (eg. site of an old long stay hospital) and photographing this. This can generate further discussion which can be recorded. Active visits like this may not be suitable for all adults. The life story work undertaken, like the individual it is chronicling, should be unique.

Reminiscence Work

Reminiscence work is usually associated with older people although its parallels with life story work are very close.

Reminiscence work is often done in groups. There are often props or prompts which can consist of photographs or videos from the past, clothing or household articles (also from the past). The intention is to support the person talk about their past, both in terms of employment and personal life (right back to childhood).

Reminiscence work helps confirm a person's identity and reinforces their individuality. It has been seen as a practical application of Erikson's eighth stage of human development, giving the person the opportunity to review their life, address unresolved questions etc.

In reminiscence work, there is usually no individual book kept (which is one difference from life story work). However, staff could support a service user generate one if the service user wanted one.

Louisa works in an older people's home. Many of the residents are experiencing confusion and depression. Louisa and her colleague Gladys talk to their manager Sanjeet about running a weekly reminiscence group to help alleviate some of the resident's feelings of loneliness and despair. Sanjeet agrees and Louisa and Gladys set up the group work. They get some CDs of old time music and some memory box items from their local library. These prompt lots of discussion and laughter in the sessions and Louisa and Gladys notice that residents also interact with each other more generally.

Individual Staff Behaviours and Attitudes

There are many examples where individual staff recognise and respect the identity of service users. Examples include:

- using the form of address the service user prefers
- finding out the service user's views, likes and dislikes and responding positively to this
- respecting the service user's family and friends and facilitating contact
- supporting the service user extend their range of experiences (if they want to)

- respecting the service user's preferred routine and ways of doing things

Identity and Recording

The way care staff and support workers record information is important since other staff will pick up on the images and messages you convey. In one service I worked in I read the daily contact sheets of a man. The main impression I got was "Know my bowels, know me". Would we like our identity reduced to this?

Staff need to be conscious of what they write and how they write it. There are various examples of recording that can positively convey identity. The assessment and care planning process should acknowledge individuality. If the care service (domiciliary care, day service or care home) develops its own care plans, do these convey individuality? In what way is the individuality of the service user conveyed so that their care plan has words or comments that are different to other care plans?

The other key example of recording is in the daily record or contact sheet. Does this convey the personality and character of the service user or does it convey the manner in which staff label the service user (by focussing on challenging behaviour or medical aspects etc)?

SECTION THREE: BEHAVIOURAL THEORY

We would argue that there is now a 'behavioural school'. The basic tenants of behaviour theory have been applied in a variety of ways. Each specific application has got its own name and approach. Some 'classrooms' of the behavioural school are described in this section but this listing is not exhaustive.

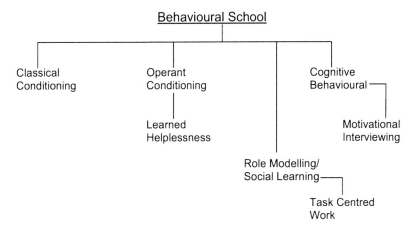

Reading this section, you will learn more about:

- Conditioning
- The ABC approach
- Social learning
- Role modelling
- Task centred work
- Cognitive Behaviour Theory (CBT)
- Motivational interviewing
- Behaviour that challenges services
- Gentle teaching
- Eclectisism
- Offending behaviour

CLASSICAL CONDITIONING

This was the original 'scientific' development most well known through Pavlov's dogs. This was where dogs were given food at the same time as a bell was rung. After a short while, the dogs would salivate when the bell was rung even though no food was presented. The application of classical conditioning to social care is relatively limited, though there are instances where staff could come into contact with this approach. One example is where a child who persistently wets the bed may have a sensor under the groundsheet of the bed. When the sensor detects urine, a buzzer or alarm sounds. This wakes the child. After a short while the child should wake when their bladder is full without the need to urinate in bed.

OPERANT CONDITIONING

This has had a significant influence in psychology and in one form or another is used regularly in social care.

Skinner (1971) was one of the original researchers but his approach has been further developed. Operant conditioning recognised that the environment (both human generated and natural) has an effect on our behaviour.

One of the insights of operant conditioning is that it highlighted many behaviours occur randomly (we just do something or say something from out of the blue). Whether we do it or say it again will be strongly influenced by the response that we get. If we get little or no response, we may not do it again.

One example is a young child who says "I want to kill myself". This can shock a child's parents. The young child may not have any idea how to commit suicide and may not fully understand what they are saying, but whether the child says it again could be dependent on how the parents or adults around the child respond to the comment.

Operant conditioning also highlights that most behaviours are a response to a stimulus. To try to capture the processes involved in how behaviour is influenced or shaped the A:B:C continuum was developed.

'A' stands for 'antecedent' – an event happens and as a result the person engages in a behaviour, 'B', which is a response to 'A'.

Immediately, or soon after the behaviour, the consequences (C) occur.

ABC charts have commonly been used in social care services. Many services have developed ABC charts so that they try to understand the broader environment a person lives in.

> Mohammad has learning disabilities and doesn't communicate verbally. Staff in the residential service where Mohammad lives find his behaviour can at times be very challenging – he is aggressive and throws things around the lounge of the service. Following the advice of a psychologist staff start to use an ABC chart – they quickly ascertain that about 90% of the time this behaviour is linked to when a particular service user is in the room. It appears that Mohammad is simply trying to communicate that he doesn't like this service user.

It is through operant conditioning that knowledge around behaviour being shaped by rewards has been developed. Rewards (or reinforcers) should be identified that the person actually likes and values. The reward should be:

- applied consistently
- as immediately as possible after the desired behaviour occurs

If part of the reward is intrinsic to the person (internal sense of pride, achievement etc) then this is helpful. Many rewards are external to the person and can include the full range of rewards we all like, such as:

- food
- money or gifts
- social companionship/praise
- activities the person likes

Some activities lend themselves to having rewards that automatically follow on eg. preparing food or drink, the reward is the enjoyment of the food or drink.

Potentially social praise and companionship is a very significant reward and this should not be under estimated.

Where a desired behaviour is complex or demanding, breaking it down and having rewards that are provided for each stage should result in the behaviour being achieved.

Jas is a family support worker. She is offering support to Rachel who has 3 young children. Rachel is struggling to manage her children's behaviour. Drawing on her understanding of operant conditioning Jas shows Rachel how to set up and monitor a rewards system. Rachel learns how to use a star chart consistently to promote positive behaviour.

SOCIAL LEARNING/ROLE MODELLING

One of the principle writers of social learning is Bandura (1977). Like so many theories, this is just describing a common life event.

Social learning describes the way that we engage in a behaviour because we have seen another person engage in the behaviour and that other person benefited from the behaviour (or they avoided something unpleasant happening to them). Social learning is more likely to be successful if the role model has status or standing with the learner and the new behaviour can be rewarded. Arguably, much of what we learn is through role modelling. This is most apparent in a parent/child relationship but there are lots of other examples.

Many teenagers and young adults learn social skills (and dating skills) from their peers through social learning. Many adults have learned other skills (such as computer skills) through watching others succeed at the task (usually their young child!).

Many self help groups and mutual support groups work on the basis of social learning and role modelling. Just one example is that of the Expert Patient Programme (EPP) (run in England). In the EPP, individuals with a long term health condition go on a training course where they learn how to manage their own condition as much as possible. One of the trainers is a person with the condition.

Mrs Bateman has recently been discharged from hospital. When she was discharged she was given several boxes of different types of medication. Soon after returning home, a social worker visited Mrs Bateman whilst the social care worker was there. The social worker asked "You're OK with your medication, aren't you?" The social care worker thought Mrs Bateman's "Yes" lacked confidence.

Later the next day, when the social care worker was with Mrs Bateman, she became quite talkative and said "I can talk to you." Mrs Bateman said she had struggled with her medications but didn't feel she could tell the social worker. Mrs Bateman said she had been visited by a friend who showed her a medipac which she uses.

Mrs Bateman realised how helpful it was. The friend said her daughter got it from 'somewhere'. Mrs Bateman asked the social care worker where she could get one; so long as she knew where to go, Mrs Bateman said she could get it herself.

TASK CENTRED WORK

Sometimes Task Centred Work is described as a theory in its own right but really is an applied approach using behavioural theory at its core.

Task centred work is often used when working with individuals who have relatively good independence skills. Two of its characteristics are that it is focussed on problem solving and that it is short term and time limited.

The worker should assist the service user to identify the problems and difficulties that they are presently facing. From a potential list the service user should be supported to identify which problems are their priorities (what is causing them the most anxiety).

Only a small number of problems should be identified. This is to make the whole task manageable. The worker and service user should agree how each of the problems is to be addressed. The focus should be on the service user recognising what they can do (in practical terms) and making a commitment to carry out the task.

One mistake commonly made is that there is an assumption that task centred work relates to the tasks the worker has to do (eg: phoning another professional on behalf of the service user) – this is not the intention.

Task centred work expects that the worker and service user will agree a date to review progress (when they next meet?).

One of the aspirations of task centred work is that by successfully completing a task, the service user will have a sense of achievement. This will be intrinsically rewarding as well as solving a problem in the person's own life (which will also generate a sense of benefit for the service user).

Additionally, task centred work predicts that once the person has had a problem and solved it (with the support of the social worker or support worker) then the next time the same or a similar problem arises, they will be able to address the problem themselves.

Anton is a young person preparing to leave care. He is working with Keith, a personal advisor on the leaving care team. Keith has a few meetings with Anton to discuss his goals in life and what sort of plans he has for moving on. Keith and Anton then work together on prioritising goals and detailing what needs to be done to achieve the goals. Anton and Keith then agree who will do what and set a date to meet again in a couple of weeks to review progress.

COGNITIVE BEHAVIOURAL THEORY (CBT)

Some writers would argue that cognitive behaviour theory (CBT) is distinct from behaviour theory but in this text we consider CBT to be part of the behavioural school.

The cognitive aspect of CBT refers to how we think. CBT rightly points out that we can consciously direct our behaviour. CBT

---

recognises that we can have long term life goals (successful job, fame etc) but to achieve that goal we have to work towards it. In working towards the life goal we may have to engage in activities that we would not want to do. A simple example is that to be a doctor, a person has to spend five years as a University student where they are basically poor and they live under the constant demand of having to pass exams or be thrown off the course. Medical students endure this because they look forward to the status and financial benefits of being a doctor.

Hence CBT recognises that we are willing to engage in short term disadvantage if we feel we will benefit in the longer term.

Arguably we start to develop a cognitive behavioural approach in our pre-teens (however there are examples of young children agreeing to endure something they dislike for a significant gain later). Whilst at secondary school, we should start to realise how we will benefit in the future as a result of doing school work.

CBT can often be relevant to adults receiving social care services. Supporting an adult move towards independence, either through acquiring new skills or re-learning skills that have been lost, can often involve care staff conveying to the service user why the service user needs to do the tasks themselves (as opposed to the staff member doing the task). The long term goal is the service user's independence. As with all behavioural theory, the reward (aim) must be the person's own aim. If the service user sees independence as a code word for being lonely in a flat by themselves then they may not want to learn the skills.

Motivational Interviewing

This is a very applied form of Cognitive Behavioural Theory. It originated in services for people with drug and alcohol addictions. Staff found it difficult to engage service users and there were only a small percentage of service users who moved from their state of addiction to actively seek to end their dependency. This model (motivational interviewing) was developed and has since been widely applied.

Motivational interviewing involves the worker having an empathic, non confrontational approach. Aspects of the technique include:

- Education about the situation the service user is in. If they are a drug user then information should be provided about the effects of substance misuse and this should be in an accessible manner.
- The staff member should encourage the service user to list the benefits and costs of their present lifestyle or situation. This should be concretely expressed (written down). The benefits and cost of an alternative lifestyle (if the person were to change their behaviour) should also be listed.
- Exploring barriers to potential goals. The staff member should support the service user recognise that there will be difficulties but many or all of these can be addressed. Again, it is best to be as concrete as possible and list the difficulties and state how each will be overcome.
- Reframing past events. When discussing barriers, it could be that the service user said they "tried that before and it didn't work" or similar. Past experiences may need to be explored and viewed from a different perspective. This reframing of past events is a key cognitive (thinking or ideas) skill. For example, if a person was a drug user and they said they tried to give up before (many times) and it didn't work, then rather than the 'didn't work' being emphasised the worker could point out that the service user has shown the determination to try and that it appears to be a heartfelt goal of the service user to give up.

Like many models or applied techniques, motivational interviewing is a blend of theories and models. In this case a blend of cognitive behavioural theory, person centred practice and counselling skills.

Motivational interviewing has been considered so useful that it is extensively used especially with looked after children (and young people leaving care), offenders and people who are homeless.

Matthew is a 16 year old looked after child who is living with a foster carer. In recent weeks the foster carer has found money going missing and Matthew is staying out late without letting the carer know. The foster carer says she cannot carry on like this much longer.

A support worker visits Matthew and gets him to list all the good things about being in his present accommodation and all the things he would need to consider if he were to leave now.

> The support worker makes the list as visual as possible, using writing and simple line drawings.
>
> The support worker makes clear what the foster carer has said. As a result of the meeting, Matthew realises the benefits of staying where he is. The foster carer reports that the situation has settled down.

BEHAVIOUR THAT CHALLENGES SERVICES

The reasons why one individual engages in challenging behaviour could be very different from why another person engages in challenging behaviour. Whilst recognising this, the basis for many people's challenging behaviour is often framed in terms of difficulties in communication and behavioural approaches.

The Function of Challenging Behaviour

From a behavioural perspective, behaviours which challenge services serve a function for the individual displaying the behaviour. The function could be any one of the following:

- To have social contact
- For self stimulation
- To resist or refuse unwanted demands
- Material reward
- To communicate something the person is concerned about (eg. they are ill)

This list is not exhaustive and so there could be other reasons.

Forms of Challenging Behaviour

Behaviours which challenge have been grouped into types, or forms of challenging behaviours. This is then given the academic term topography. The forms of challenging behaviour include:

- Aggression
- Self injury
- Disruption and/or screaming

- Destructiveness towards property or items
- Inappropriate social responses (eg: sexualised behaviour)
- Running away
- Over activity

One of the difficulties is that any one form of behaviour (eg: self injury) appears to serve different functions at different times. Potentially it could serve several functions at the same time.

From a psychologist's perspective, the way to work with an individual who has behaviours which challenge is to work out what functions it is serving (and it could be many) and then address these through behavioural techniques.

Any care plan for an individual could have various elements to it. One of which could include supporting the individual communicate their wishes through the use of symbols or signing. The staff team would have to respond positively to this which would be a double re-enforcer for the service user in that the service user gets what they wanted (social contact or to be left alone or get a drink etc) as well as realising that they can control their life by communicating through using signing or pictures rather than engaging in behaviour which challenges.

Values, Belonging and Trust

At various times writers within learning disability services have reacted against what they perceive to be the clinical (cold) approach of psychologists from the behavioural school. Broader, looser reasons for why people display behaviours which challenge have been suggested. These include:

- A sense of alienation and profound isolation (who really loves me, who can I trust?)
- Anger at the sense of powerlessness experienced by the service user

In response, writers have raised the importance of not covering the person in the blanket of the label 'challenging behaviour'. It is important to see the individual as a person with personality, identity and all that this includes.

One example of this approach was 'Gentle Teaching' (McGee 1985 and 1992). The effectiveness of Gentle Teaching has been hotly debated (eg. Mudford 1995). One point that is worth carrying over is the importance of recognising the humanity of the service user and for those around the service user to connect with them and not to just coldly grant or withhold rewards in pursuit of a reduction in one type of behaviour or another.

Self Injurious Behaviour

There has been increased interest in self injurious behaviour over the last 15 years or so. This is partly because it has become clear how relatively common it is and that it occurs in children, teenagers and adults.

Again the potential reasons for self injurious behaviour are many.

- In some people who have experienced great emotional hurt, the emotional pain is so great the person needs a physical 'site' to 'explain' the pain. This can result in head banging, cutting or other self injurious behaviours.
- Self cutting can become self reinforcing as the body releases it's own opiates (pain relievers) when cutting occurs
- Self injurious behaviour is functional (as referred to above) and the behaviour is maintained through reinforcement (probably unintentional reinforcement by staff or family members)

Self injurious behaviours can represent a particular challenge since it quickly touches on our own values. Staff who work with individuals who engage in self injurious behaviour will probably benefit from training and detailed information (which is beyond the scope of this introduction).

ECLECTISISM

Being "eclectic" means using a range of theories in any given situation. Essentially it is the approach that most people take most of the time – it's very rare for someone to be simply working on the basis of one theoretical approach. It is perhaps in working with behaviour which challenges services that staff take the most eclectic approach.

To illustrate this eclectic approach, we will first consider one very specific behaviour which services find very challenging (pica) and then move on to the more general area of offending behaviour.

Pica

Pica is the name for the behaviour of eating non food items. Pica has been well documented. It is considered developmentally normal until a child is aged about 18 months old. There are cultures where clay is eaten at certain times for specific reasons. Individuals suffering malnutrition have been known to consume soil and coal.

Within care services pica behaviour has been recorded in learning disability services and in services for older people who develop dementia (although the occurrence of pica in this group is relatively rare).

In exploring and addressing pica, staff need to explore a range of theoretical approaches:

Psychological Theories

Psychological approaches view pica as a learned behaviour. Some writers have claimed that it is self reinforcing as a result of the oral stimulation it produces. There is also some evidence that people engage in pica more in environments with less social interaction. Some researchers claim pica is a form of aggression (Ali 2001).

Medical Theories

There are various possible medical causes for pica.

1. Mineral deficiency. Possibly the most promising route is the evidence that indicates people who engage in pica have iron or zinc mineral deficiencies. When individuals have been given mineral supplements, incidents of pica have reduced markedly (although not necessarily down to zero).
2. Neurological and neurochemical causes. There is some evidence that brain damage and diminished neurotransmission may result in pica behaviour. Some individuals who develop dementia start to have altered eating habits and a small number of people with dementia start engaging in pica.

3. Psychiatric disorders. There is some evidence that mental health issues could result in pica but this appears to hang on a relatively small number of cases.
4. Nicotine Addiction. One feature that has been noted is that many individuals who display pica can be particularly focused on eating cigarette butts. It is likely that the pica behaviour resulted in a range of non food items being eaten. This would include cigarette butts. As a result, an addiction to nicotine was established and the individual recognised that cigarette butts satisfied the addiction and so they take the opportunity to consume cigarette butts whenever possible. The use of nicotine patches has been suggested to address this.

Offending Behaviour

Identifying the reasons why people offend immediately leads to a consideration of theory.

In the past (even the relatively recent past) the main emphasis on addressing offending was to approach it using behavioural theory.

In the 1980s under Margaret Thatcher's Government, youth offender prisons adopted "a short, sharp, shock" approach. If a person commits a crime then they will have an unpleasant experience (both being in prison and being in a prison with a tough regime). This (so the theory goes) will deter the person from re-offending,

Psychologists who supported behavioural theory did not agree and argued that such an approach misrepresented behavioural theory and was bound to fail. Behavioural theory requires any punishment for an action to occur straight after the action occurs, otherwise the connection is lost. Also behavioural writers argued that you need to consider the person's environment. When the offender leaves prison, what are they going back to?

In recent years the emphasis has been on adopting a broader more eclectic approach. It has been identified that people who offend have multiple problems. These problems include:

*   difficulties with accommodation (person is homeless or only short term accommodation)
*   person has drug or alcohol problems

- person has social network and family problems (conflict, ruptured relationships)
- unemployment
- poor educational attainment
- possible mental health problems

Another perspective is to consider people who don't offend. Why does a person not offend? The simple answer is they are getting all their needs seen to, they are enjoying their life and if they offended they would put all the good things in their life in jeopardy.

In this sense behavioural theory does explain why people do not offend. Even if a person has not got everything they want at a particular point in their life, they don't offend because they think they can achieve their goal at some point in the future (eg: to buy a house, then work and save money etc).

Since people who offend have many problems there have been two additional approaches:

- Try to stop young people offending in the first place. Give them a sense of opportunity and positive stimulation: drawing in many ways on theories of human development – specifically Maslow's hierarchy of needs.
- When a person is offending, address each of the problems they have. This draws on various theories. Hence if a young person has conflict with one or both of their parents, then one consideration has to be attachment theory. If attachment issues are part of the problem then the parent(s) will need to convey that they do love their son or daughter. Their parents may benefit from parenting classes. If there are education issues such that the young person does not fit in at mainstream school and is at risk of being excluded, then moving to an alternative education provider may be an option. Alternative education providers use groupwork to good effect and often also address some of the other problems a young person may have.

Multi-agency working has also been a strong re-occurring theme in recent years. The intention is that through multi-agency working the different problems a person has can be addressed. Also the person is supported in a clear and consistent manner.

Using an eclectic approach (drawing on different theories) is likely to be more effective that relying entirely on a simplistic application of behavioural theory.

SECTION FOUR: POWER, POWERLESSNESS AND EMPOWERMENT

It is essential that people working in social care have a well developed understanding of power and powerlessness.

Most staff do not automatically perceive themselves as in a position of power, although they may recognise the power people have over them. In many ways this is indicative of how power operates – people recognise the power others have but not always their own power.

Reading this section you will learn more about:

- Power
- Powerlessness
- The care/control debate
- Empowerment
- Advocacy

POWER

What is Power?

In this book, power is defined as:

"Having an effect or influence over a person such that they carry out an action that they would not have carried out if they had not been under that effect or influence."

Using this definition means power and violence are different. In many ways, when violence occurs, it is a sign that power has not been accepted. However, some powerful people or groups just use violence to express their absolute power (as a way of saying "I have hit you and you can't do anything about it.").

Power is rarely concrete and immobile. A person or group who are powerful cannot keep that power for ever.

Power is also about the nature of a relationship between at least two people (one powerful compared to the other) or between groups of people (eg: nation states).

The balance of power can therefore move in a relationship. A person who is at first very powerful over another person may start to lose some of their power due to, say, the less powerful person starting to assert themselves and refusing to do what the powerful person instructed them to.

A power relationship is likely to be stable (where one person is powerful and another person less powerful) for two reasons:

- Firstly, the powerful person may have the ability to apply sanctions to the less powerful person if they refuse to do what the powerful person has instructed them to do. (An employer could apply disciplinary measures to an employee; a parent could withhold love and affection from a child.)

- Secondly (and arguably more importantly), the person who is less powerful consents to the arrangements as they exist (and so does not try to rock the boat). People who are less powerful consent for a number of reasons. These include:

- a belief that the more powerful are better than them so should rule (eg: the aristocracy are better than workers etc)
- the less powerful feel they do benefit from the way society is ordered
- no sense of alternative or no confidence in any possible alternative

Whenever you meet with someone, there is a power relationship. If you meet with friends, the power relationship is likely to be evenly balanced. If you meet with a senior manager, it is likely to be heavily tilted in the manager's favour. A person who is parent to a young child has a huge amount of power over that child.

As mentioned already, power relationships are not static. A friend may become more powerful if they become Robbie Williams personal assistant! A manager's power is limited to certain matters relating to work. If she or he tries to go beyond those limits or they act inappropriately, then the employee who is less powerful could start a grievance procedure. The parent's power over their child will lessen as the child becomes a teenager and the teenager asserts their own autonomy (the power to decide things for themselves).

Whenever a social care worker meets a service user, there is an immediate power relationship. In social care services, the power relationship is influenced by the following factors:

Power held by the service user

- The service is meant to be for the benefit of the service user
- The service user has the right to complain if not satisfied with the service provided
- The service user may have other people to turn to for support (eg: family member)
- Personal qualities of the service user eg: articulate, confident, educated etc.

The service user's perception of their own power may be undermined by:

- One or more negative experiences that have markedly reduced their confidence

- A profound sense of vulnerability due to the fact that they are dependent on the social care worker, which inhibits making complaints
- A lack of knowledge of their rights
- Isolation
- Previous attempts at claiming power over their own life have failed (learned helplessness)
- The person may have their ability to express themselves impaired by mental health issues or a learning disability

The social care worker will be powerful by comparison to the service user. Possible reasons for this could include:

- Possible age, gender or race of the social care worker compared to the service user (eg: thirty year old white woman supporting a black woman in her 70s).
- The social care worker has a role or a job to do. This is heightened if the worker presents as busy, with lots to do.
- The care tasks are one way, the service user needs care support, not the worker; the worker knows lots about the service user etc.
- The social care worker is one of a team and has the power to influence the viewpoint of team colleagues through recording or team discussion

A social care worker's perception of the limits of their power may be influenced by:

- The social care worker's professional values which prompt them to show respect for the service user, recognise that service users are experts of their own situation etc.
- The knowledge that service users could complain about them
- Awareness of the presence of colleagues and of regular supervision from line manager

Most social care workers have significant power compared to a service user. When social care staff offer choices to service users, the manner of the presentation and the selection of options represents the application of the worker's power.

Service users may pick up from staff what answer they feel the staff member is wanting the service user to give and so comply with this.

We need to maximise service user autonomy and so staff need to be conscious how they are using their power. Are staff using their power to enhance the service users independent decision making skills or to guide the service user to an option that is easy for the staff and the service to respond to?

Sources of Power

Raven (1993) listed five types of power, some of these apply to social care workers, and some will apply to managers or other professionals eg: social workers or community nurses.

- Legitimate Power. This is power that exists due to the way an organisation is structured or society is ordered. An Assessor has power over an NVQ or SVQ candidate in terms of deciding if a piece of work is adequate. A social worker can decide if a person is eligible for a service etc.
- Expert Power. This is where a person is seen as having a bank of knowledge or expertise. A benefits advice worker is one example but there are lots of other examples.
- Reward Power. This is power gained through the ability to give rewards. In social care this is most likely to occur if a person is isolated and health or social care staff are the main contact points for the service user. The service user will only get any sense of reward (social contact) from health and social care staff.
- Referent power. This is power created by the admiration and respect a person can have for another. This is probably most likely to be encountered in terms of the service user's respect for their G.P. (although the G.P.'s power is also derived from legitimate and expert power).
- Coercive power. This is power based on the ability to apply punishment or sanctions. This power is most keenly felt in childrens services (going to court for a care order) and mental health services. The service user could be conscious of this power even if it has not been actively applied by social workers.

It is important to recognise that in addition to these five sources of power, there is societal power. As we have covered in Section One some people experience oppression at the hands of others. Oppressors are powerful, oppressed people are less powerful. So for example, an older person who experiences ageism will feel less powerful than a younger person.

CARE AND CONTROL

With power comes responsibility. Social care and health services need to use the power they have in a responsible manner. The care and control debate has been one of the main arenas where professionals have considered "How do we use our power responsibly?"

Childrens services have wrestled with this question throughout the 1990s and into recent years. For direct support staff the focus has to be on care. We need to enable the service user, say a young teenager, to feel wanted and valued. If that service user continually puts themselves at risk by running away then social care staff need to accurately record and report this so that social workers and other professionals can consider alternative options (which is where the control will come in).

In adult mental health services the same principles apply. The direct support staff should focus on providing care. If a person's mental health deteriorates the social care workers knowledge of the service user can be an important prompt for other professionals to introduce more control.

Part of the care environment is shown by social care workers making clear to service users the possible consequences of their actions. Boundaries are important for all of us.

POWERLESSNESS

Some service users can maintain some power over their own life, possibly because they are articulate or have active family support or make full use of direct payments etc.

Many more service users experience a significant sense of powerlessness. The service user is likely to have been through significant changes in their life, most of which were unwanted. They may have acquired a disability or mental health problem or may have been subjected to abuse. Having contact with social workers and social care workers can be difficult for some people to adjust to. If the service user has had to move into a care home then this can be a profound change. Often the decisions the service user is still able to make are relatively minor. The service user has little real say over key decisions. The service user probably didn't want to develop mental health problems or to acquire a disability. The child didn't want to be abused and taken into care. This can result in the service user having a profound sense of powerlessness. The attitude of the staff, the way the service is organised and the ethos can all influence whether this sense of powerlessness is heightened or reduced. Many service users feel powerless and their lack of confidence (due to the knocks of life) is likely to result in a sense that they are unable to change their life in the way they would like to. If the service user develops the view that they cannot change anything because they are powerless this is termed 'learned helplessness'.

Stan has learning disabilities and limited verbal communication skills. On the whole he is very withdrawn and has little social contact. A new keyworker (Paul) is allocated to work with Stan. Paul is conscious that Stan does not have the opportunity to communicate his wishes. In Stan's file Paul finds an old communication therapy report that recommended the staff start a Picture Exchange Communication System (PECS) with Stan. This was never done. Paul pursues this. He establishes contact with the communication therapist and his enthusiasm wins the support of the manager. Paul presents the PECS system to the team. He conveys that he feels Stan is withdrawn since he feels powerless. If he can communicate and if staff act on his communication, then he will engage more. Paul says that Stan will be given a number of cards with simple drawings on eg. A cup of tea; TV; sandwich. When Stan hands one of the picture cards to a staff member they must respond (eg. Get a cup of tea; assist him put the TV on etc.) As a result of the staff using the PECS system, Stan became far more active in the house and less withdrawn.

EMPOWERMENT

Empowerment is about the service user having choice and control in their own life. However, empowerment recognises that this is easier said than done and so it goes on to outline what needs to be in place for the service user to be able to take control.

Empowerment has become a very significant concept within the last twenty years or so. Arguably this is because there has been an increasing level of honesty and realism in respect of services.

For years social care services and health services were intended to benefit service users. On the whole, in say the 1970s and 1980s, services cared for people but provided care services in large buildings (either residential or day services). The care was largely institutional and service users had to fit in.

As the quality of life of people in the general population rose, so the expectations of those receiving care services started to rise. Sometimes carers and family members were significant because they felt the services available were not good enough for their loved one.

Added to this were reported incidents of abuse and misuse of power by staff towards service users. A new realism arose in the late 1980s that care services were not good enough. The very services that should be upholding and valuing people were not doing this. Care and health services were actually contributing to service users sense of powerlessness. Decisions were made by organisations or by professionals that directly affected individual service users; where options were available they were often few in numbers and more of the same (that large care home or that larger care home?).

Empowerment theory makes clear that it is not enough for professionals to just say "Okay, we'll let the service user decide, it's over to you, take it away!".

It is possibly helpful to think of a person who is powerful (a politician in power, a wealthy person etc). They will probably have had the opportunity to receive a broad education; they will have experienced successes in their life, such that they have a certain confidence; they will have people around them who can give them information; they have access to resources so that what they want can be worked towards etc.

When this powerful person is compared to a service user, it should become clear that there are great differences. The service user may, or may not, have had a good, broad education. The service user may well have experienced rejection or discrimination such that their confidence is undermined. They are not likely to have an entourage of officials. In fact, a significant number of service users rely on benefits, so they will have very limited resources. Additionally, the service user may have emotional problems (eg: a teenager with attachment issues) or mental health problems or dementia etc.

Empowerment theory (and practice) recognises the need to address each of these areas (and others) as well to give the service user any true chance of making decisions about their life.

Helping Service Users to Develop Resources

One of the starting points is to acknowledge that the service user is the expert about their own life and where they want to get to. This does not mean the person will make what is objectively the most sensible decision. There are lots of people in the general population who smoke, drink too much alcohol, live in accommodation that is not 'right' for them (a house that is too big or too remote etc).

From here services need to support the person develop a range of resources. These include:

- Information: This should include information that is broader than simply what services are available. Information may need to be provided about the person's past, or their condition (if they have a condition). All the information should be available to the person in an accessible manner.
- Network of support: Who is there to provide emotional and moral support? Who can the service user express their frustrations to knowing that the listener will still help them renew their resolve and determination?
- Skill development: In a status and class conscious world, it's not always what we say but how we say it that counts. The service user may need to learn various social or technology skills (eg: using e-mail); how to shape their argument and list points so that the person they are addressing is aware of why they need to listen to the service user.
- Confidence: Service users need to have the confidence to want to express themselves. To young confident people, it may seem surprising to learn that there are many individuals whose confidence is so low that they say little or nothing about decisions that effect them and they 'go along' with the dominant person. Confidence building can be a difficult and slow task. Ways to enhance confidence include joining with others who have had similar experiences and have successfully changed their life

positively; the individual chooses an aspect of their life they want to change and there is a good chance of this being achieved; when the person raises their concern they have a supporter present.

- Having a voice: This follows on from many of the preceding points. When a service user expresses something about their own life, services should listen. In the past, services were so poor at listening that the advocacy movement developed. Therefore having a voice may involve having an advocate.

- Problem solving approach: The service user will need to recognise that practical difficulties could arise in seeking to change their own life in the way they would like to. To achieve their goal, they will need to adopt a problem solving attitude. For every problem there is a solution.

- Resolve: Individuals need to recognise that services and groups of professionals can have an inertia and inflexibility that is surprising considering the fact that services are meant to help service users and professionals are, on the whole, keen to listen to service users. A service user who wants to change the way a service does something so it meets her or his own needs will need a great deal of personal resolve. This is a personal quality but it can be supported by a social network, the provision of information etc.

- Resources: Most of life's achievers already have practical, financial and other resources. If a service user is to achieve their goals they will also need resources of one form or another. The idea is that social care services will provide the resources. In practice, social care services are too tied up in existing brick and mortar services. When a service user has care needs but wants to continue their present lifestyle then established services struggle to provide the flexibility needed. Interestingly the introduction of direct payments partly addressed this. Direct payments, arguably, represent one of the most practical tools for empowerment provided by social care services.

Within adult services, the success of direct payments has resulted in the Government of England pursuing similar initiatives such as Individual Budgets. Individual Budgets are intended to provide the service user with a pot of money that they can use flexibly to meet their needs. The money could be used for access to employment, housing support etc.

Practices and Attitudes

As well as supporting the service user develop the skills and resources necessary for them to feel empowered, services also need to address some of their practices and attitudes.

Social care services are seen as the "Be all and end all". Too often staff and professionals view a service user being 'received' into social care as the goal. This attitude has to be addressed. Social care services should be the invisible support that enables a person to get on with their life and do the things they really want to do. For service users their life goal may be: contact and involvement with family; cultural and social activities more extensively; education; voluntary work; employment. For too many service users, entering residential care is like entering a monastery. It becomes their world.

Risk and Empowerment

One important aspect of empowerment is that it acknowledges the dignity of risk. In the past, opportunities for adult service users were restricted because of anxiety about risks to the service user. If anything there is still a split between adult and children's services. Children services struggle to reduce risks, adult services could allow more risks (clearly this is a generalisation; take it for what it is worth).

There are many examples where adult services have got better at managing risk. Often the risk management plan is decided through multi-agency meetings, involving the direct care staff, professionals from outside the service and the service user. Such an approach can enable the adult service user to live the way they want to even though there is significant risk.

Where no multi-agency meeting has been held then direct care staff and mangers of a service can feel anxious about allowing risk. It is important that a multi-agency meeting is convened otherwise if the direct care team doesn't allow risk, the service user can feel disempowered. If the direct care team allow the risk and something goes wrong, then the care team could be criticised.

In social care, acknowledging and managing risk is an important aspect of empowerment.

copyright© Kirwin Maclean Associates

Hopefulness

Many of the people we support have had their confidence so extensively undermined and have experienced so much discrimination and stigma that the road to empowerment is long and slow. This means social care staff need to develop an attitude of hopefulness and recognise that the service user may make a commitment to do one or more things but the person does not follow through or relapses.

Staff need to avoid becoming cynical and dismissive about the service user when the service user next expresses a desire to change some aspect of their life.

A looked after teenager may say he or she is going to start to attend school but this resolve starts to falter. Staff need to find ways to visit this aspect, again, without cynicism.

An adult drug or alcohol user may join a rehabilitation programme but then relapse. This should not be used as a reason to dismiss the service user's interest in coming off drugs or alcohol in the future.

There are lots of other, less significant, changes in lifestyle that a service user may express a commitment to address. When the service user does not achieve their own (attainable?) goal, then staff need to be respectful. The service user may not even be honest to staff about not achieving their goal. Such honesty could make the service user feel stripped of all dignity (they have failed again). Good staff will enable a service user to have a sense of their dignity whilst maintaining an honest dialogue.

To avoid situations where staff members hopefulness appears superficial, then it may be more helpful to describe the professional quality as realistic optimism. The service user could well find any planned change demanding. But it is possible.

User Involvement

Organisational structures that facilitate service user and carer involvement are vital in terms of empowerment. Social care services need to 'build-in' service user and carer involvement into their structure and decision making process. Services need to evaluate whether they are doing a good job and a key aspect of this is what the service users think. Therefore services need to regularly find out from service users how they experience the service.

All services need a comments and complaints procedure and this is one aspect of gaining some sense of service user views but on its own it is not enough.

Services need to have regular, planned involvement of service users. This can take various forms including:

- Managers having regular meetings with a self advocacy group
- If there is a management board then service users or carers sit on this board
- If there are plans to develop or alter a service, then service users or carers sit on the sub committee or planning group
- The involvement of service users and carers in the training of new and existing staff.

These are just some examples. Some social care services give the impression of being more developed than other services. Arguably children's services involve service users (or former service users) in decision making better than adult services. Some services for adults with mental health problems and some services for adults with physical disabilities have also demonstrated how service users can be involved. Progress in services for older people and adults with a learning disability has been patchy.

Putting it Together

Empowerment is a developed concept. It requires an acknowledgement of how disempowered service users can be. To enable the service user to feel truly empowered, the service user needs to be supported onto a platform (or springboard) from which they can move. Empowering practice involves:

- Recognising power differentials
- Listening and hearing
- Seeing people as experts on their own problems
- Helping service users to develop resources
- Developing positive attitudes and practices
- Acknowledging the dignity of risk
- Encouraging hopefulness

- Facilitating user involvement

ADVOCACY

Advocacy is a widely accepted principle of good practice. In many ways, though it now has a significant history within services, advocacy is often implemented in a half-hearted way with a lack of real commitment from services and staff teams.

Essentially, there are two different forms of advocacy:

Self Advocacy

This is where the individual refines the skills they already have to speak for themselves; often self-advocates join together to form groups, both to gain a sense of personal support and to have more of an impact on the services they receive.

Self advocacy is about enabling and empowering people to act on their own behalf. There is no doubt that this is a powerful way of helping people achieve independence, although it might not be feasible for all service users. Often assertiveness training is needed, helping people raise their confidence and sense of self-worth, and teaching the skills necessary to make other people listen.

Many services now have self-advocacy groups. If staff limit their understanding of self-advocacy to the people who are members of such groups and to the topics discussed in the group they misunderstand the aim of the whole advocacy movement. People should be listened to as they express their views and make decisions about their own life and the services they receive on a day to day basis.

It is the failure of staff and services to listen to people, ordinarily, that has resulted in the rise of the self-advocacy movement.

Citizen Advocacy or Professional Advocacy

This is also known as independent advocacy. This is where an individual enters into a partnership with a service user with the intention to clearly express what the person is communicating. Citizen-advocates are usually volunteers (unpaid). However, increasingly advocates are employed by advocacy services – hence the term professional advocacy.

It is not the job of the citizen-advocate (or professional advocate) to say what they think is best for the person they have got to know. Their task is to convey what the service user is trying to say even if they disagree with what the person is saying.

Independent advocacy is important because most service users find themselves compromised in one way or another in terms of expressing their own views:

- There is a strong power imbalance in favour of the authorities
- Individuals may be lacking in confidence
- They may not have the verbal or other communication skills to express clearly their own meaning
- Their families may not agree with their own views and may put pressure on the person

An advocate can help someone work out exactly what they want, if necessary and then challenge services on that person's behalf.

Sometimes confusion reigns as to who can be an advocate. Strictly speaking, any person working for an organisation, which provides services or goods to an individual, cannot act as that person's advocate. This is because an employee unavoidably has competing loyalties. Also, some of us find it hard not to impose what we think is best for the service user, and would genuinely struggle to present the service user's own views as paramount. We need to recognise this and allow someone else to take on that role on behalf of the service user.

The Limits of Advocacy

One of the central dilemmas of advocacy has been that a citizen advocate or professional advocate requires the service user to express their view. This raises two questions. Why does that person need an advocate? and (more importantly) what about service users who cannot express themselves clearly? To answer the first question, the service user who can express themselves needs an advocate either for reasons of moral support or because services haven't listened to the service user up to now.

The more important second question has received various answers. Some advocates feel that they can identify what a person is seeking to communicate even if they have no clear language. The advocate will observe the service user and try and gauge from the service user's facial expression, body language and any vocal sounds or simple words what the service user likes and dislikes. Sometimes the advocate will draw information from people who know the service user well (family members, direct care staff) and this will be used to create as full a picture as possible. By spending time with the service user and observing them (this is sometimes called a "watching brief"), the advocate hopes to be able to get to a position where they feel they can express something of the service user's viewpoint.

Some advocates argue that such a "watching brief" is open to interpretation by the advocate and so decline to be involved.

We are left with the situation that some very vulnerable people, who don't have clear communication skills, are left almost completely voiceless.

> Dorothy is an older woman who is supported at home by domiciliary care staff. After a brief stay in hospital following a fall Dorothy's two sons contact the domiciliary care manager saying that it is vital that their mother goes into a residential home "Where she will be nice and safe." Dorothy doesn't want to go into a home but she doesn't want to upset her sons either. She asks a support worker what she should do – she doesn't feel able to tell her sons how she feels. The support worker tells Dorothy about a local advocacy project. Dorothy gets in touch with the project who provide a volunteer advocate to support Dorothy express her views at a review to be held in a couple of weeks.

SECTION FIVE: WORKING WITH STRESS AND DISTRESS

Social care staff work with stress and distress on a daily basis. This section explores some of the theories about this area. Whilst much of this will relate to your work with service users, you may also find it interesting in terms of your own feelings and emotions.

Reading this section you will learn more about:

- Stress
- Stress management
- Stress vulnerability model
- Grief and loss

STRESS AND STRESS MANAGEMENT

Stress could be described as a situation where a person perceives that the demands being placed on them are greater than their personal resources can cope with. The person feels they are stretched up to, or beyond, their personal limit.

One of the difficulties with describing and considering stress in the modern world is that some people use the term 'stress' to mean any demand or any change they encounter, no matter how small it is. This is one reason why the opening definition refers to the person's own perception and their own feelings. One young twenty something adult I know appeared to have a life crisis over deciding where to cross the road. For her the walk to University was stressful!

It is commonly accepted that many people work and perform better if they have certain demands placed on them. Most people like some form of stimulation or a challenge. That challenge could be anything from running a marathon before the year is out or raising one or more children to become well adjusted adults.

This has resulted in the inverted 'u' or the 'n' being used to represent the situation where people perform best with a certain level of demands placed on them, If there are too few demands the person may drift or float, but if there are too many demands, the person starts to be overwhelmed.

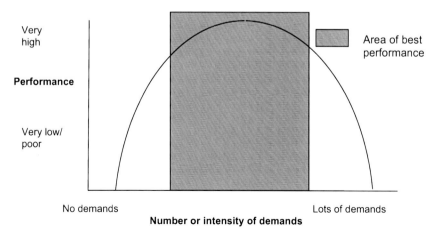

Peoples Reaction to Stress

Some demands on us do result in the classic fight or flight response. The body produces adrenalin. This may be helpful but it is a short term response. It may also be unhelpful since the adrenalin can result in a person being less calm (agitated) and possibly more likely to get angry.

In the medium term the body and mind can deal with significant demands. However, if the demands are very intense, even for a short period of time, the person can develop a post traumatic stress disorder.

If the demands are less intense but still significant and long lasting then the person can develop burnout. They become drained, or spent.

Stress Management

The main responses in dealing with stress are well known:

- Make use of your social network. If stress is work related then make use of your professional network, colleagues, line manager, other professionals etc. If the stress is from personal demands, then ask for support from family members and friends.

  As part of this, a person needs to be honest. Especially in terms of personal life. If the demands are too much, tell the person. If children are being too demanding, tell them!

- Food, sleep and rest. When many demands are placed on us, it is more important to eat well, get good sleep and to rest. A person will not perform as well if they are tired and hungry.

- Attitude, problem solving and prioritising. It is glib to expect problems to disappear by pretending they are not there. But problems may be solved by a variety of means. If a person looks at a problem from different perspectives they may find a solution. Sometimes the problem may be our own making. The teenager who is defying their parents may be right. Maybe the parents are being too restrictive and should let go a little.

We may have a long list of demands. But are there some that can wait? Are there some demands that if dealt with now will prevent a problem from escalating? Only deal with a few demands at any one time.

Stress and stress management relates to both staff and service users. It is easier to tell others that difficulties they face need not be seen as overwhelming until the same difficulty effects us and we are overwhelmed.

This should not stop us from helping people recognise the ways they can improve their stress management skills. In the same way it should not stop staff from recognising that it is from service users that we can learn how to deal with the every changing demands of life.

> Michelle has moved to full time work (having been a part time worker for the last few years). Michelle feels that the expectations on her are too high, with her partner still expecting her to do all the child care and household chores.
>
> Michelle discusses her concerns with her partner Malcolm. At times the discussion is heated. As a result Malcolm agrees to make use of his employers flexi-time and pick the two children up from school one day a week. They also decide to take up the offer from Malcolm's mother to pick the children up from school two days a week. The children are to go to a child minder for the remaining days. Additionally, Malcolm agrees to take it in turns with the main household food shopping. Michelle also gets agreement that one night a week is her night out since Malcolm plays football every Sunday. All of this support helps Michelle feel less anxious and less stressed.

THE STRESS VULNERABILITY MODEL

The Stress-Vulnerability Model was originally generated by Zubin and Spring (1977). This model puts forward the view that some people develop mental health problems when they feel under stress and their coping mechanisms are not able to manage the intensity of their own stress.

There are various factors that influence whether an individual is at risk of developing mental health problems because of stress. The factors include:

- Biological predisposition. It appears that some people may be more prone to developing mental health problems compared to others. There may be a genetic aspect to this. However, it does not mean a person is definitely going to develop a mental health problem, even if they have a genetic predisposition.
- Experiencing stressful events. As covered, stress could be described as experiencing personal demands that are perceived by the person as greater than they can cope with. They are stretched beyond their limit. Stressful factors can accumulate. If a person is already experiencing poverty or difficult social relationships then individual events can result in the person feeling overwhelmed. Examples include illness in the family, birth of a child etc. Some events can be so significant that even if the person is 'comfortable' then they are overwhelmed eg: being a victim of crime or bereavement.
- Coping skills. Some people have good coping skills. Good coping skills are partly shown through the person's attitude and outlook and partly through problem solving skills.
- Social network. Having an active social network that the person can draw on reduces the impact of stressful life events.
- Positive role. Having a positive role is known to be important to the vast majority of people. If a full or part time job isn't appropriate, then voluntary work or a role at a day centre can be beneficial.
- Professional support. This can consist of opportunities for counseling or having medication prescribed.

A person's genetic predisposition cannot be altered. Therefore the main benefit of this model is to assist staff and service users focus on the other aspects of a person's life that can be worked on.

GRIEF AND LOSS

Models of grief and loss outline the experiences that people go through following a significant loss.

The loss or bereavement may be anticipated or unexpected.

Some writers argue that people progress through recognisable stages. Other writers claim that people's responses are more fluid.

Accounts of grief and loss apply to bereavement (someone important to the person dying) and loss (a person experiencing a significant change that they didn't want such as losing a job, acquiring a disability etc.), although experiences of loss can be less intense.

Models of Grief

Kubler Ross (1969) argued that there were five stages of grief, these being:

- Denial. On first hearing of the person's death there may be disbelief. The person may hang on to the hope that the deceased will walk in as normal. Numbness and shock may also be felt.

- Anger. The strength of the pain results in anger; this anger can be directed at anyone, including self anger where the bereaved person blames themselves.

- Bargaining. Some people may try to negotiate with another person or with God to be given another chance, to be able to go back to how things were before.

- Depression. Once the person starts to absorb the full truth they may become deeply saddened. There can be intense feelings of loneliness and hopelessness. The person may be tearful over minor matters. They may have no energy for routine activities.

- Acceptance. There is no requirement that the deceased person is forgotten, but the bereaved person needs to recognise the truth of their situation and to gradually release their emotions. They will need to realise that they can carry on even if they still feel the loss of their loved one.

Bowlby (1980) has characterised the grief process as more dynamic. Bowlby listed four experiences but aspects of all of them could be experienced by the bereaved person within the same week in any order. The four processes are:

- Shock and numbness. Although this process is most likely to be felt soon after the person is bereaved, it may be delayed due to the person feeling they have to be strong (for the sake of others).

- Yearning and searching. The bereaved person may look for their loved one. There could be experiences where the bereaved person is sure they saw or heard the deceased person. This process is sometimes referred to as 'pining'.

- Disorganisation and despair. This is the process that includes the emotional turmoil that engulfs people who are bereaved.

- Reorganisation. The bereaved person starts to accept the loss they have experienced and will need to establish their identity afresh.

These are just two models, but there are others. Even though these approaches claim to be different, there are many similarities between them.

There are other models of grief. Some add additional stages; others claim there are three or four stages.

Behaviours and Emotions

The range of behaviours and emotions that people experiencing grief and loss display, are extensive. All the literature makes it clear that the individuality of the grieving process is to be respected. The pain can be intense where the relationship was very close; a person could feel relief if the relationship with the deceased was destructive.

Added to this is the cultural view of grief. In some cultures, grief is very expressive and public; there is an expectation that the bereaved will be in company for days to share their grief. In other cultures the importance of privacy is emphasised.

The length of the grieving process is also very individual. However, it is to be hoped that the bereaved person is able to function within four to six weeks of the death of their loved one, even though their emotional state may still be very raw.

Loss

As mentioned earlier, the grieving process is also relevant to situations where no one has died but a person has experienced a significant loss of some form. Examples could include:

- The unwanted ending of a love relationship or divorce

- Being made redundant

- Acquiring a significant disability as a result of an accident that results in various life changes

If you were to look again at Kubler Ross' stages and Bowlby's processes, then these can also be seen as relevant to a person who has experienced such an unwanted change.

This has relevance for all residential care staff where a new resident (a teenager or an older person) has entered the care home due to circumstances that were largely unwanted or against their wishes.

It is also possible that some people develop mental health problems due to loss or bereavement or that a person who already has mental health problems is very adversely affected by loss or bereavement.

Salvador, aged 15, was hit by a car and his doctors have said it is unlikely he will walk again. Salvador played football and was in the football academy of the local premiership football team.

Since the accident, Salvador has had periods where he has been very angry and resentful. There have also been times when he's said he'll teach himself to walk and run again.

When Salvador returns home, his parents indulge him. However, they are surprised he is so withdrawn; he used to be so outgoing. A health care assistant, who is involved in follow up, explained to the parents that Salvador is going through stages of loss.

SECTION SIX: THEORIES ABOUT SOCIAL CARE PROVISION

The theories and models covered in this section relate to the way that social care is provided. Some relate to specific aspects of work which staff may not see as relevant to their own practice. However, it is important to remember that much can be learnt from theories about the way social care is provided in different ways.

Reading this section you will learn more about:

- The Medical Model
- The Social Model
- The Recovery Model
- Groupwork Theory
- Social Role Valorisation
- Service Accomplishments
- Insitutionalisation
- Person Centred Care
- Holistic Approach

THE MEDICAL MODEL

The medical model has developed since the mid 19th Century.

The starting point of the medical model is the ideal human body, in looks, physique and health.

- One development of the medical model idolised the perfect body and this resulted in the eugenics movement of the late 19th Century and early 20th Century. The eugenics movement argued that only the fittest nations, made up of healthy, fit people could complete in the world. The health and fit (non-disabled) should have children.

  The eugenics movement argued that people who had a disability or impairment, or a mental health problem or some other perceived social failing should not have children since their children would be the same and society would be swamped. If a disabled person entered state care, they were kept in segregated services, with no opportunity for romantic or sexual relationships.

- Another development of the medical model did not go as far as idolising the human body but it emphasised a 'normal' or 'acceptable' physique. A person's impairment, disability or mental health problem is a deviation from the normal and needs to be corrected.

- The individual with the disability or impairment or mental health issue is the problem. This problem needs to be cured or corrected.

- The impairment, disability or mental health problem is viewed as intrinsically bad or undesirable. Having a disability is seen as suffering a personal tragedy. This aspect when seen separately, is referred to as the tragedy model of disability.

- Knowledge and expertise is located within the medical profession (doctors). They know what is best for the person. This knowledge is made inaccessible to others by a language that is confusing. Words or phrases include:

  - Diagnosis – what is wrong with the person
  - Prognosis – likely outcome eg: cure or learn to live with the condition.

- Aetiology – cause or origin of illness
- Pathology – change occurring due to illness or disease

- The disability, impairment or mental health problem has to be diagnosed. This is a form of labelling. The label is viewed very negatively in society.

- The person with the impairment or disability or mental health problem has to fit into society (as it is) and if they can't, then they are excluded or removed.

THE SOCIAL MODEL

The social model of disability was generated in the 1970s and has progressively evolved. Aspects of the social model include:

- The concept of 'normal' is misleading and unhelpful. Instead there should be recognition that diversity is part of our human condition.

- The social model draws a distinction between impairments (a recognition that a part of the body is not functioning) and disability. A person with an impairment is disabled (prevented from doing things) by society.

- Society disables people due to viewing their impairment negatively and then comprehensively discriminates against people with an impairment.

- People with a physical disability have been made invisible or ignored by society. Buildings were built so that people had to be able to walk to get in them.

  By contrast the development of the car was seen as desirable. Buildings were built so cars could get onto the sixth floor of a building (multi storey car parks) and huge areas were made accessible to cars (road building). This shows that if society wants to, it can make buildings and locations accessible.

- The social model has made clear that society can make itself accessible to all people and disabled people have a right to equal opportunities.

- The social model has worked to counter the negative stigma associated with the labels applied to people. This is in a similar way to how other liberation movements have worked. For example, gay pride has been mirrored in the disabled people's movement.

- Within learning disability services the stigma of the label has been so difficult to shake off that one theme has been "Label jars, not people."

- The importance of not reducing people's identity to a label has been emphasised. One disability rights campaigner was Glynn Vernon. He asked onlookers to say what they thought his problems were. A possible answer was "A quadriplegic who can't talk properly." Glynn's view of his own problems was "I don't have enough money and I don't have enough sex."

- The social model has championed the expertise of the individual. Only the person themselves knows what is best for them. This can be particularly important where someone has medication, since side effects can be very individual.

Continuing Debate

Many people merge aspects of the medical and social models.

Many doctors recognise the limitations of medication and other medical interventions. It is not unusual for a doctor to enter into a discussion with the patient as to what is the best way to proceed. There can be more shared decision making.

Unfortunately there are many social care staff who are in awe of the medical profession and its power. If social care staff are working with a service user who they find challenging, it is not unusual for the staff to look to a doctor for a cure or at least relief (in the form of medicating the service user).

Social care staff need to maintain the view that many service users who challenge services have experienced broken relationships and powerlessness. As such, staff could base their response more on the social model rather than the medical model.

The Application of the Social and Medical Models to Service User Groups

People with a physical disability have been particularly active in promoting a social model perspective. The introduction of legislation making it a duty to maximise access is a sign of the success of the disability movement. This shows that if society wants to, it can make itself accessible. However, some people with a physical disability also acknowledge the strengths of the medical model – if they experience pain for example, they may value the involvement of medical staff and their advice about pain management.

People with a learning disability have not been as successful as people with a physical disability. There has been progress but much still needs to be done.

In mental health services, the differing medical and social perspectives are, arguably, most keenly felt. The medical perspective uses language that creates barriers eg: psychosis, schizophrenia etc but claims benefits through the use of medication. The social perspective on the other hand argues for recognising diversity (many of us hear voices to one extent or another) and the benefit of talking therapies (eg: counselling). Also the alternative causes of mental health problems such as poverty and abuse are highlighted.

In children's services, the label of Attention Deficit Hyper-Activity Disorder (ADHD) has generated a new area of debate. Is it a medical condition or a child's response to their environment (for example, poor and inconsistent parenting, sense of (in) security and stimulation/ activity)?

In drug and alcohol services there has been a debate for many years about whether a medical perspective or a social perspective is more helpful.

It is worth remembering that homosexuality was considered a diagnosable illness and was only removed from the World Health Organisation list in 1992. In Britain in the 1960s gay men were subjected to painful aversive treatments to 'cure' them.

copyright© Kirwin Maclean Associates

A mental health service user group arranged a social event which includes a rock band. Some of the songs written by the lead singer are about his mental health problems. Also at the social event is an opportunity for people to deliver their own poetry.

On the day of the gig and the social event a petition is sent round calling on the local council to increase the height of the walls at a bridge in the area since two people have committed suicide from the bridge in the last two years.

One of the poems read by one of the poets describes the side effects of his medication and how he found counselling far more useful.

THE RECOVERY MODEL

The recovery movement has developed since the 1990s, although it can trace aspects of its roots back further. The recovery movement is a counter to the view that of all those with long term enduring mental health problems a third would need continual psychiatric care (with a significant death rate through suicide), a third would need intermittent psychiatric care and a third would be able to lead relatively ordinary lives, with support, after a period of poor mental health. The recovery movement points to an increasing body of evidence that 50% to 68% of individuals make a complete or near complete recovery.

The recovery movement has no set conditions but common aspects include the following:

- Finding someone who will hold a "candle of hope". People who achieve recovery relate the importance of having people around them who continue to hope and conveyed a sense of confidence that recovery would eventually occur.
- Refusing to be called or referred to by their diagnosis eg: 'schizophrenic'. The individual needs to remind themselves and others that they are a person and not an 'illness'.
- Changing one's attitude to conditions. This can include individuals deciding not to 'collaborate' with their label.

- Developing attitudes of self reliance, personal responsibility and countering internalised sense of self loathing, shame and fear.
- Recognising the strengths and abilities of individuals.
- Finding meaning and purpose despite the persistence of symptoms. Recovery does not mean an individual will, say, never hear voices again.
- Healing from the effects of the stigma and discrimination. Finding ways to return to work or education etc.
- Empowerment. The development of a person's sense of control over decision making in their own life is vital to recovery. Professionals need to respect the individual's expertise about their own situation.
- Peer support, mentoring and guidance. An effective and supportive social network.
- Additional support to those who have experienced trauma and or abuse and for those who have drug or alcohol addictions.

Psychiatrists who support the recovery movement would also place the importance of observing drug treatments in this list. Many service users would as well, although they may place drug treatments within a framework of receiving information about drugs and entering into a discussion with mental health professionals about exactly what drugs are most beneficial for them.

Chi has mental health problems. He has a number of options in terms of day time services. For example he could go to the local hospital day service where they have groups on anxiety management, art therapy etc. This is a very medical model led service. There is also a local drop in facility run by a voluntary organisation, where service co-ordinators encourage service users to engage in local community activities, go on outings etc. This is a service led by the social model. There is also a local service user led group which meets in different venues twice a week. This is facilitated by service users for service users. It is based on a recovery model approach. Chi feels he could gain from all three services, so he attends each of them for a couple of sessions a week – choosing what he wants to attends through discussion with his support worker.

GROUP WORK THEORY

Group work theory is important in social care since care services use group work so much. Group work theory can be separated into two parts. The first is describing what is going on in terms of relationships within the group (group dynamics). The second aspect is the benefits and disadvantages of group work.

Social care services use groups a lot. Groups are used for a number of reasons. They include:

- Services may form groups because group care is easier and cheaper than individual care. A care home where there are more than two people is effectively drawing on group work. Many day centres and day services provide group care.

  This type of group care is at risk of having significant tensions. Group work works best when the group has some voluntary aspect and there is a strong shared need or aim. Group care is often an expression of the service's need for a smooth running routine and so service users can't be said to volunteer for the group. The shared needs are often quite broad eg: a group of looked after children in a care home or older people with confusion in a day centre.

- Group work for meeting educational or learning needs. Where several service users have similar learning needs then group learning can be a more effective approach than one-to-one learning. Group members may prefer the social aspect to group learning.

- Group work dynamics are part of an intensive learning process. This is partly related to the point just above. Some agencies intentionally use group work because group work is likely to be more successful in achieving the goal of behaviour change. Examples include agencies that set up groups for people who offend; for people who have a drug or alcohol addiction etc. Part of the group work process is to engage in mutual critical evaluation. In other words, if a drug user is engaging in denial then other members of the group will be able to point it out, as they won't be fooled.

- Group work can be a key part of the process of empowerment. One of the key ways that oppressed individuals can counter discrimination is for people from the marginalised group to join together, recognise their common experiences of discrimination and to jointly take action against the discriminations. Group members can also gain from having their identity positively valued; receiving mutual support etc.

This list illustrates some of the reasons why group work is relatively common in social care services.

Group Dynamics

There have been many writers who have discussed group processes and group dynamics. Arguably the most famous is Bruce Tuckman who coined the phrase "Forming, storming, norming and performing" (Tuckman 1965).

In Tuckman's theory, the stages refer to:

Forming. This is concerned with how the individual members of the group start to orientate themselves to the group. The individuals test out boundaries in respect of any leaders in the group and other group members. New relationships of dependency and interdependency are started.

Storming. This is a period of conflict around interpersonal matters and perspectives. The conflict is a form of resistance to the group and resistance to achieving the group goal. Groups can go through the 'storming' phase more than once, especially if new members join.

Norming. This is the stage in which the conflict is successfully addressed. The group develop its own identity, individuals are able to express themselves and the new roles are accepted.

Performing. In this stage, the group actually starts to successfully work towards the group task. The energy of group members is now spent on achieving the group goals. Individual roles in the group can become more flexible and functional.

In 1977 Tuckman and Jensen added a fifth stage.

Adjourning. This relates to the end of the group and the end of roles that individuals had in the group. This stage highlights that individuals can experience a sense of loss when a group finishes.

Tuckman's account of the stages groups go through has been extensively referred to. It should be recognised that not all groups go through these stages. However, many people involved in group work feel Tuckman's account is useful and can be commonly seen in group processes.

Benefits and Difficulties of Group Work

Groups often form when individuals have something in common and the task is so significant that people realise it could be beneficial to form a group. In social care the 'common theme' that the service users have often relates to having a similar identified need.

The benefits of group work include:

- Individuals can have a sense of relief that they are not the only ones in a certain situation. Whether it is parents trying to manage teenagers or adults with a drug or alcohol dependency, meeting with people in a similar situation generally gives individuals a sense that they are not alone. The individuals can also feel able to express themselves fully, since they are with people who, broadly speaking, understand their situation. This too can be a source of relief and release.
- Individuals can learn from other group members techniques for dealing with a particular difficulty (using a role modelling/social learning approach). Sometimes comments from other group members are respected more than comments from professionals (who may not have experienced what the group members have lived through).
- Individuals can develop a positive role and feel able to contribute. This means the individual is no longer in a dependency relationship; there is an equality or mutual dependency to the relationship.
- Group members can develop insight or reflective thinking. Effective group work involves openness to being challenged. Comments from other group members can be the means by which individuals realise why they have recurring difficulties or are not progressing. Comments from group members can often be better received than comments from professionals. Some types of group

work expect group members to be critical of each other (eg: in groups for people with drug or alcohol dependency).

- Group membership can help individuals develop a positive sense of identity. This is partly related to the first point but more creative. People who are ordinarily in a minority can find great benefit from meeting with people who have a similar identity. People from specific minority ethnic communities can gain much mutual support from meeting together to celebrate their shared identity (eg. Poles, Kurds etc). It can also be beneficial for various service user groups eg. teenagers leaving care, self-advocates who have a learning disability etc.
- Attitude change is notoriously difficult to achieve. Group work is considered one of the methods that is most likely to result in attitude change. This can be significant when the group consists of, say, sex offenders.

The difficulties of group work include:

- Attitude change. Sometimes groups are used to change attitudes 'the wrong way'. The Nazis and other extreme groups use group process to advance their own goals.
- Societal inequalities are mirrored in the group. Group work is intended to be a safe forum in which group members can address the problems they face. However, it is easy for groups to have within them the same prejudices and barriers that are found in wider society. In a group with men and women, do the men dominate the group and make comments that undermine the women? In a group that has only one black person, is that person at risk of being excluded?

There are various means to counter this. One is the establishment of ground rules which explicitly bar sexism and racism, but group members then need to enforce the ground rules themselves.

Where there is a group facilitator, they have a responsibility (along with group members) to raise concerns about discrimination that is occurring in groups.

Sometimes groups are specifically formed for people with similar identities and backgrounds eg. a mental health group for Asian women, to try to avoid this happening. Even then however, there can be dominant individuals who may need aspects of their

behaviour addressing since they can have a negative impact on the group.
- Group work has limits. Group work is intended to be beneficial for all people in the group. However, some individual members may not find the group that helpful. Group work nearly always involves an element of compromise. Group work seeks to address shared needs; on the whole it does not address individual needs that are experienced by only one group member.

In adult day services and residential care homes, groups are often formed for social activities. However, one person in the group may not want to do the planned activity. Such an individual can be viewed as awkward. Labelling such an individual as awkward or selfish is not helpful. In many ways the 'awkward' person is conveying that they are an individual and they are only in that group since that is the way services work. Services often get round this situation by making it clear that participation in social groups is voluntary.

Staff at a Children's Centre set up a group for young parents in the local area. The group provides education about issues such as play, child development etc. It also provides an opportunity for parents to meet and develop their social networks. Ultimately some members of the group help to set up a new group which is arranged to specifically consider the needs of teenage mothers.

SOCIAL ROLE VALORISATION

Social role valorisation (previously known as normalisation), is a development of the principle of normalisation first expressed in Scandinavian countries in the late 1960s. One of the main writers who has helped to develop Social Role Valorisation is Wolf Wolfensberger (1983). See also Wolfensberger and Thomas, (1983).

Social role valorisation/normalisation began in learning disabilities services. However in recent years, it has been more widely applied and is now seen as applicable throughout social care.

There are seven themes to the principle of Social Role Valorisation (SRV). If you think of SRV as a parent with seven children, all of

---

whom do and say different things but together make up a family, this gives us an idea of the way in which the seven themes work together.

SRV is made up of language which on the face of it is jargonistic and difficult to understand. However, once we look beneath the jargon it is very easy to see how the principle of SRV and the seven core themes relate to social care practice. Whatever you do, don't let the language put you off – work through each of the core themes and look at applying them to your day to day work.

1.   The Role of (Un)Consciousness in Human Services

For us to begin to look at what this first theme means in practice, carry out the following exercise:

Think back to your childhood and try to identify the first time you came into contact with someone who had either a physical disability or a learning disability. It may be that you have *always* known a person with a disability (for example a family member) in this case think back to your earliest memories of them. Alternatively, you may remember isolated examples such as seeing a person using a wheelchair when you were out etc. Whatever the situation was, think about how you felt and what you did at the time. Remember this is about when you were a child, no one is going to judge or assess you on the feelings you had then or on what you did. You must be as honest as possible for us to look at this theme effectively.

What you might find, as you reflect back, is that one of the feelings you had was curiosity. Children are often curious about people with disabilities. As a result of this curiosity they ask questions, of the person themselves, their parents, a teacher etc. If you have contact with children yourself you may have heard the kinds of questions – *"Why does that man walk like that?" "Why does she look like that?"* etc. The problem comes when adults don't give reasonable answers to these questions. Children might be told *"Shush – stop looking. I told you not to stare"* or *"He's very poorly"* or *"She's no different to you or me"*. Of course these answers are the start of some of the other feelings you might have identified – if you were told as a child that someone was "poorly" – you might feel sorry for them (pity); on the other hand if you were rushed away and told not to look you might have begun to feel afraid.

This is known as the process of socialisation. Our early experiences often form our values and feelings and very often these are negative. If we are honest, we will have a mixture of feelings towards the people we work with and these may change over time, or in terms of context. These current feelings may not always be respectful and positive and some of them may be influenced by our earlier experiences. For example, if you are supporting a person in an unpleasant personal care task you may feel disgusted, even physically sick. If a person has been aggressive towards you, the next day when you come into work you might feel apprehensive, even fearful. Feelings are a part of all of us.

What this theme is saying is that both individuals and society in general, carry negative feelings towards people who need care services. These are usually unconscious and can be formed throughout our socialisation. Since human services are staffed by individuals and form part of society, these feelings can be expressed through service delivery. It is a stated aim of SRV to be honest about unconscious thoughts and processes within services, so that they can be directly addressed.

After all, if you are a carpenter, working with a piece of wood the way you feel about the wood will not have an impact on your work – but if you are working in social care, then you are working with people, and the way you feel towards them will have a profound impact on your work.

This theme carries one of Wolfensberger's brilliant insights. Society values some qualities (eg. young adult, attractive, wealthy etc) as positive and views some qualities as negative (ageing, physical disability, learning disability etc). The qualities society views negatively it feels it cannot be honest and explicitly negative. So society's negative view goes into the societal 'unconscious'. Society masks its dislike of people who are different by creating services that are meant to 'care' for the people who are viewed negatively. But these 'care services' have an unspoken (and primary) goal of keeping people viewed as different and deviant away from mainstream (valued) society. The explicit goal of care services (to help service users) is only their secondary goal. Since society considers the people in the services to be unimportant the services are poorly resourced. Hence the quality of care is at risk of being poor. Therefore Wolfensberger's brilliant insight was that traditional care services are part of the oppressive structure that service users face.

Care services need to be honest about their origins and the need for them to change before they can adequately support service users become valued members of society.

A direct access hostel for homeless people has been poorly managed for several years. A new manager arrives. The new manager is aware that some of the bedrooms are shared, resulting in vulnerable people mixing with street wise people. The rooms for women residents are not securely separated from the other rooms. The staff apply rigid rules on eviction for minor matters and wholesale eviction when drugs are found. The manager says that all the service is doing is making local people think that there is a service for homeless people so all rough sleepers are there of their own accord. The service is not resolving homelessness at all.

As a result, the manager develops a plan to move all the homeless women to a separate women only house. All shared rooms are to be phased out. Staff receive new training on key working and how to engage service users by using motivational interviewing. New pathway plans are developed with a focus on assisting the homeless person get their own accommodation.

Some staff are really keen on the changes. Other staff are dismissive and say that the service users don't deserve better than they currently have.

---

2.   Role Expectancy and Role Circularity

This theme is very closely related to the processes of stereotyping and labelling, which are covered in section one. It is basically what is often known as the self-fulfilling prophecy.

The idea is that individuals who are already valued will have positive experiences and high expectations will be placed on them, which they will strive to fulfill. Individuals who are at risk of devaluation will have fewer demands placed on them, and expectations will be low and stereotyped. There will therefore be little motivation, or encouragement, to excel or reach their potential. This may have the effect of, for example, denying or withholding opportunities because people are not expected to benefit.

Most people have experienced this to one extent or another themselves. For example, when the British education system was based on 'O' levels or C.S.Es a teacher would make a decision about what each pupil could achieve and they would be assigned a role/class etc based on this decision. Many people who experienced this, or who experienced the eleven plus system, feel that they never reached their full potential in school because of peoples low expectations of them.

Many parents of people with learning disabilities may have been told by doctors when they were born that "they'll never do anything" etc. This may have been said thirty years ago and still be having a profound impact on the opportunities given to people. We all know people with learning disabilities who are quite independent who, for example, are not allowed to make a hot drink by their parents.

The following diagram demonstrates the cyclical nature of this situation:-

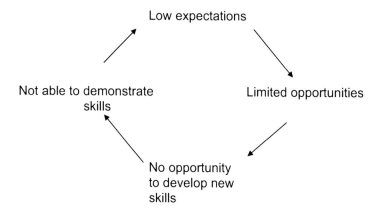

A further example of role expectancy may be where an older person who has perhaps had a stroke and lost certain skills is seen as lacking the capacity to re-learn these skills or learn different ways to do something.

3.   The Conservatism Corollary

Of all the language used in terms of the seven core themes this is probably the most jargonistic. It is nothing to do with party politics.

To help us to begin to look at what the conservatism corollary is, work through the following exercise:

Read through the following list of statements:-

- Spending most of my spare time colouring pictures
- Having a bank account
- Owning a car
- Living with six other people I hardly know
- Watching television
- My parents knowing all the intimate details about my personal life
- Having a paid job
- Being able to go out until late
- Choosing what to wear
- Eating meals at set times (by the clock)
- Going out with people who talk to each other but not to me
- Being able to nip out to the shops when I've run out of something I like
- Having a set bedtime
- Having someone to choose all my clothes
- Choosing what to eat and when to eat it
- Owning my own home
- People talking about me in my presence – but not letting me join in

Now think about these from your own position not in terms of the people you work with, and divide the list into things you value for yourself (i.e. you would like them to happen to you). Things you don't value (you wouldn't like to happen to you) and things you don't mind (no strong feelings).

If at all possible, discuss this list with other people - it doesn't really matter *who* - just discuss the list with other people.

Would they have placed the statements under different headings i.e. do they value/not value different things?

Now consider again what you value/don't value. Does anything strike you about it?

One thing that usually happens when people carry out this kind of exercise is that the things that they wouldn't value are the kind of things that happen to people in receipt of care services on a regular basis. Just as examples:-

Living with six other people I hardly know

Most people would not particularly value this. However, for many people living in residential services this is often the case. They may be living with many people that they hardly know – certainly they wouldn't have known the other people when they moved in together.

My parents knowing intimate details about my personal life

Most of us only tell our parents (and anyone else for that matter) what we want them to know. However, for many people with learning disabilities, even very detailed information may be shared with parents. For example, parents may know details about a woman's menstrual cycle, details about their adult son/daughter's intimate relationships etc.

And as a final example:-

Having a set bedtime

Most of us would value the option to choose when we go to bed – perhaps watching the late film sometimes and having an "early night" on other occasions. However many people in receipt of care services are given set bedtimes. For example, for people living in residential services, although most services (thankfully) have moved away from set bedtimes, many people have become institutionalised and will still prepare for bed before the night staff arrive. Alternatively people living in residential services may be actively encouraged to go to bed at certain times (sometimes because of staff convenience). People in receipt of home care will have a set time when the care worker visits to help them to bed. This can be unusually early because of the need for home care staff to visit many people each evening.

On the other hand many of the things that the wider population do value are out of reach of many people in receipt of care services. To take just a few as an example:

Choosing what to eat and when to eat it

Most of us value this – we don't always, for example, want a full evening meal, we might want to eat earlier or later depending on what we have planned for the evening etc. However, for many people living in residential services this isn't an option. When there are a number of people to eat, sometimes we can't get away from set meal times, some limited choice may be available but this would not be to the same extent as other people etc. Again people in receipt of home care will have set times when care workers visit to support them with meals.

Being able to go out until late

While many of us may not do this on a regular basis, most of us value being able to do so if we choose. However, many people do not have this opportunity – if they live at home their parents may not allow them to stay out late. If they live in a residential service they may go out in the evenings, but it is likely that they are not able to stay out after say 10.00 p.m. because of shift changeovers etc.

Having considered this area in some detail we can return to look at what the conservatism corollary says. This theme is also informally known as the positive option. Essentially it states that people who are at risk of devaluation will be further devalued unless the *most* valued social role/activity/relationship is offered and experienced. As services, we often fail to seek the most valued life experiences for people. We should always strive to use the most positive images and activities in service delivery to enhance the status of service users.

What can be difficult in this area is that we all value different things, as you will probably have discovered if you discussed your list with others. It is therefore necessary sometimes to think about the majority i.e. what would *most* people value? Of course, it is also important to bear in mind a person's cultural background and general principles of diversity (for example, in looking at valued social relationships etc).

4. The Developmental Model/Personal Competency Enhancement

We all continue to learn and develop throughout our adult lives. No one could say that their learning ended when they left school. This theme basically states that there must be an assumption on the part of services that through the use of social education, positive experiences, facilitation of learning, high expectations etc. all individuals can experience tremendous growth.

One of the failings of services in relation to this area is linked closely to role expectancy and role circularity. If individuals are not expected to learn it is unlikely that they will.

One of the best known messages from this theme is what has become known as age appropriateness. This theme would assert that adults are unlikely to learn when taught as though they were children. We only need to look at principles employed in colleges of adult education to see the differences between the ways in which children learn and the ways in which adults learn.

5. The Power of Imitation

Imitation is one of the most powerful learning mechanisms known – in terms of adult learning, imitation is often referred to as 'modelling'. Often people will pick up the mannerisms of their family/partner because they are living together and begin to mimic each other. A more formal example would be the way in which new staff 'imitate' or model their behaviour on more experienced staff.

This theme of SRV states that positive role modelling should be capitalised on by services for the benefit of service users.

6. The Dynamics and Relevance of Social Imagery

This theme is covered in detail in section one. See pages 16-21.

7. The Importance of Personal Social Integration and Valued Social Participation

Basically, this is referring to the segregation which people in receipt of social care can face. This theme states that services should seek to counter this segregation of individuals and groups. However, social integration must work alongside social participation. Since the run down of the old institutions (eg. hospitals for people with learning disabilities and psychiatric hospitals), some of the services which have replaced them have largely become mini-institutions in the community.

It is vital that as well as living in the community, people take part in their local community. Where people are only physically integrated and not *personally* integrated lip service is being paid to SRV.

SERVICE ACCOMPLISHMENTS

Service development in response to SRV has been variable. Unfortunately various professionals have not always understood some of the main points made by SRV. In fairness Wolfensberger's description of SRV can be complex.

Partly in response to this other writers have sought to explain options for service development in more accessible ways. One example is O'Brien's service accomplishments (O'Brien 1980). Originally there were five but these have been increased. Often people now talk of the seven accomplishments. These are:-

Status and respect: Each person should receive a service that enhances their sense of self-esteem.

Choice: Everyone should be offered choices and supported to make choices relating to day to day and major life decisions.

Competence: Everyone should be supported to learn and develop across a whole range of areas.

Community presence: Every one should be in ordinary communities; accessing services and facilities in the same way as other members of the community.

Relationships: Everyone should have a network of relationships which include a partner, family and friends.

Individuality: The uniqueness of each individual and the need for individual self expression must be recognised.

Continuity: Each individual should experience a natural progression in their life. When change in one part of a person's life occurs care must be taken to minimise disruption in all other parts of the person's life.

INSTITUTIONALISATION

Institutionalisation is a term that can be applied to various levels of social and human relations. In terms of this book, we will focus on the institutionalisation of care services.

When care services were first developed in the late eighteenth and early nineteenth century, many of the advocates for the services had a genuine, humanitarian interest in the well being of people with mental health problems and people with learning disabilities.

Unfortunately, the early asylums were under resourced and were quickly filled. The only way to manage the services was to establish organisational practices that had as their priority the smooth running of the organisation (or institution).

The process of institutionalisation had various features, which included:

- Establishment of set routines eg: meal times.
- Depersonalisation of people; individuality is discouraged or suppressed.
- Pervasive power of the institution over the service users, including little or no privacy for service user.
- Power of staff over service users, which is effectively beyond challenge.
- Impoverished environments where only most basic needs are met.
- There was a profound stigma associated with the institution and this was applied to the people who had to live in them.
- In classic 19th Century institutions there was an expectation that service users should work and be productive.
- Classic 19th Century institutions attempted to be self sufficient (produce own food or own goods to pay for food).
- In general, institutions are closed and self contained. Contact with people who live outside the institution is limited and restricted.
- There is no real concept of development and personal growth for service users. The institution generates dependency through limiting opportunities for service users and providing all basic needs eg. food in food halls etc.

- The institution creates a "parallel world" rather than allow integration. The classic institutions had their own church, shops, work places and some had their own schools.
- Activities are all conducted in large groups. This includes visits out of the institution.
- Service users had no real choices and institutions prevented giving service users any meaningful choice.
- 'Classic' institutions also imposed strict segregation of men and women. Relationships were prohibited.
- The institutions developed abusive practices:
  - the general denial of rights was abusive
  - individual staff engaged in physical or sexual abuse of service users
  - staff could agree abusive care practice eg. excessive use of medication
  - the more powerful service users were abusive towards the most vulnerable service users
  - the ordinary quality of care was often routinely neglectful eg. incontinent service users left in own urine, smell of urine was pervasive
- There were separate facilities for staff and service users eg. toilets, canteens etc.
- There was superficial but energetic commitment to reducing risk. This was achieved through maintaining barren environments. However, average life span was no better than the general population.

Institutionalisation was intimately connected with the large brick services of the 19th Century and 20th Century. These services were wound down in the late 20th Century. This was sometimes called de-institutionalisation. Many people hoped it was the end of institutional practices. Unfortunately it quickly became clear that there was a significant risk that services develop an 'institutionalisation without walls'. Many of the features of modern institutionalisation are lesser degrees of those found in the classic institutions.

These include:

- Still no real commitment to person centred care. Care plans are all very similar.
- Service users have to fit in with service routines and staffing rotas.

- Choices for service users are still very limited, both in terms of the services available and what is provided within a particular service.
- Quality of care can still be poor. Basic care needs are met but staff are rarely present with service users.
- Group care is still a major feature of services, even when the group is as small as four people.
- Services, arguably, benefit staff more than service users and services are organised so that they are for the convenience of staff.
- When a service user has very specific needs or wants to maintain a lifestyle that is different from the service routine, then the service can struggle to be flexible enough to meet the person's needs or to uphold their lifestyle.
- There are still examples of separate facilities for staff and service users eg: toilets. The staff toilets being cleaner and better kept.

To counter institutionalisation in services, most policy documents have made clear the importance of person centred care and the inspection agencies in the UK place a high importance on individualised care. However, many services still have institutionalised aspects to them. One reason for this is that (consciously or unconsciously) staff actually like some institutional practices because it makes their working life easier.

Pawlina starts working in a small group home for adults with learning disabilities. There are only four tenants so Pawlina is hopeful that it has a homely, individual feel to it.

When she starts she's amazed to find that the taps in the bathroom and downstairs toilet have been removed. The kitchen is locked and only staff can go in. Pawlina is told that one of the male tenants kept turning the water taps on and so they decided to remove them. Staff refit the taps for baths and showers but then remove them straight after. The kitchen is locked for 'health and safety' reasons. When the staff have a tea or coffee they gather together in the sleep-in room/office, whilst the tenants are in the living room.

When discussing individuals activities, the long serving staff member says that all four tenants often have the same activities. The highlight is the disco on Friday from 8.00pm until 9.30pm at the Club! Pawlina asks if any of the tenants go to a night club in town until late. The long serving staff member says that would mean working late on a Friday night! Also the tenants prefer the disco. Pawlina wonders who prefers the present disco arrangements most, tenants or staff?

PERSON CENTRED CARE

Person centred care is not a theory; it is more an application of values into practice.

Person centred care has arisen as a reaction to institutional care practices. It has been spurred on by service users who have advocated that the service should be for them.

Person centred care is little more than the term says: the person should be at the centre of the care service.

The following are all significant aspects of person centred care. Social care staff and other professionals (eg health professionals) should:

- respect the service user
- recognise their individuality including gender, race, culture, family, lifestyle etc.
- recognise that the person is the expert on their own situation
- recognise the strengths and abilities of the service user

Therefore when a care plan is generated, it should be based on the person's individuality and lifestyle. The service user should be literally and figuratively at the centre of the care plan meeting. Staff should talk to the service user and listen to what they say. Staff and professionals should identify what the service needs to do to meet the individual's needs and not simply list what is presently available and expect the service user to fit in.

The ideal of person centred care is that the service users lifestyle continues as if they needed no care. The care and support staff are involved to assist the service user with personal care, or with getting to places or events etc.

Even if a service user enters a care home, person centred care would expect that this is used as a base and the service user still visits the people they always have done and goes to the social, educational or work activities they engaged in before entering the care home. At present, when a service user enters a care home, so much of their life has to change, contact with friends (and sometimes family) is markedly reduced and other opportunities are also reduced.

Sometimes when a person enters a care home their health and fitness is not as good as it used to be and this can also account for changes in a persons life, but too many services still rely on the new service user 'fitting in'.

Person centred care recognises that people's needs change and personal development occurs. Services provided to a person should, therefore, also reflect this. This may involve having person centred care planning meetings every four to six weeks.

Person centred care planning would also welcome the involvement of people who are not health or social care professionals. This could include old friends, neighbours etc. So long as all the people involved have an interest in promoting the service user's individuality and well being.

HOLISTIC APPROACH

Holistic care is closely related to person centred care.

Holistic care is an approach that considers the whole person. Holistic care has been a reaction against social care and social work that just focussed on an individual's personal care needs.

Holistic care requires social workers and social care workers to recognise that a person has:

- extended family not just a family carer
- neighbours and friends
- a culture and ethnicity

- a spirituality, possibly expressed through one of the major world religions
- likes and dislikes
- hobbies and activities
- a personal financial situation (rich, middling or poor)

Holistic assessment, by a social worker, draws on all these aspects as well as assessing a person's care needs, independence skills, health and medication, mobility etc.

Holistic care will seek to meet the needs a service user has by meeting the personal care needs etc but will also seek to meet the service users needs in respect of contact with wider family and friends, pursuing hobbies and interests, support the service user attend religious or ethnic events etc.

SECTION SEVEN: ADULT LEARNING

Whilst the other sections of this book have explored the theories you need to understand in terms of your work with service users, this section explores a more personal aspect. The section covers adult learning theories which will help you to explore the ways in which you can learn and develop your own practice.

Reading this section you will learn more about:

- Experiential learning
- Andragogy
- Principles of learning
- Approaches to learning
- Learning styles
- Dissonance
- Reflective Practice

Whilst the theory in this section will be most applicable to your own learning and development, you will also be able to use your understanding of these theories in helping service users and colleagues to learn and develop.

PRINCIPLES OF ADULT LEARNING

Reviewing adult learning theory and literature, it is clear that there are a number of basic 'rules' or 'principles' of adult learning, some of which are detailed below:

The Law of Exercise

People learn best by actually doing something. "Practice makes perfect!" Practicing something away from the real environment will not help someone to learn. Whilst we believe that we are helping people when we give them lots of opportunity to practice a skill, if this is not performed in the real environment with the real equipment etc, we may well actually be hindering an adult's learning.

The Law of Association

Like building anything new, knowledge needs to be built upon. New facts, skills or approaches are best learnt if they relate to something we already know, or have experienced.

The Need to Know Motivation

It is clear that adults learn best when they feel that they need to know, what they are called upon to learn. If an adult doesn't feel they need to know, they are unlikely to learn ("what's the point?" is a common question).

The Need to be Self-Directing

Responsibility for adult learning is largely individual. Adults learn best when they are directing their own learning.

The Readiness to Learn

Linking with the self-direction principle, adults will only learn effectively when they have a readiness to learn. This can relate to recognising what there is to learn and recognising why this is important and relevant. However, if these approaches to adult learning have been considered and an individual still has no "readiness" to learn, even the most effective teaching will probably not facilitate learning.

Learning Empowerment

Adults learn best from a position of confidence, it is important therefore to recognise peoples experience and facilitate some degree of self confidence. If the teaching/supportive relationship is viewed as one where the learner is the 'empty vessel' and the teacher the 'full vessel' – prepared to fill the other with knowledge, then the person learning will not learn effectively.

The Learning Environment

Research into adult learning identifies the importance of the environment for learning. Here teachers have a role in facilitating a 'safe environment' for learners. This may mean ensuring that the environment is not artificial etc.

Plateau Learning

We all learn at different rates and we may experience some good days and some bad days. It is not realistic to expect steady increases in learning patterns. Plateau will occur in our learning, though learners do not always recognise or expect this and we may need some reassurance at around this time.

Learning Continuum

Learning is a continuous experience. It is vitally important never to think you have nothing more to learn.

Positive Reinforcement

We learn best when we receive positive reinforcement. Recognition of learning is a big incentive for future learning. Specific and realistic feedback can aid reinforcement for learning.

Whole/Part/Whole Learning

Individual parts of a task, or knowledge, can only be assimilated when the whole is understood.

Memorising Learning

In using our memories to enhance learning, it is important to remember that just as people have different learning styles, so some have different memory styles. Some have pictorial memories; some have verbal memories or thinking styles. Pictorial thinkers learn best with the use of diagrams, whilst verbal thinkers learn best by reading something; diagrams, flow charts etc are meaningless to them.

EXPERIENTIAL LEARNING

Experiential learning is probably the main adult learning theory referred to in the social care arena. David Kolb (1984) is probably the most well known writer in experiential learning circles, although experiential learning can actually be traced back to 450BC when Confucius said:

> "Tell me, and I will forget. Show me and I might remember. Involve me and I will understand."

Experiential learning basically proposes that people learn based on an experience by going round a cycle of four stages. Kolb describes these as:

1. Concrete Experience
2. Reflective Observation
3. Abstract Conceptualisation
4. Active Experimentation

Along with many other theories, you can see that this is full of jargon. The following diagram shows the cycle in more straightforward language:

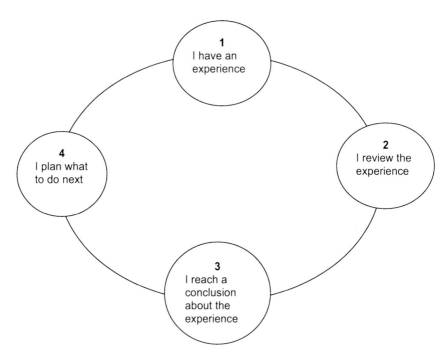

The most straightforward way of thinking about the learning cycle is to recognise that people only learn based on experience. However, the experience in itself will not be enough to ensure learning – just because you do something you won't necessarily learn from it. People have to continue round the cycle in order to learn from the experience.

ANDRAGOGY

Malcolm Knowles (1984) believes that most adult teaching has consisted of teaching adults as if they were children. He argues that adults are different from children as learners in three critical ways:

1. In terms of their self concept. Whereas a child first sees themselves as a completely dependent personality, the adult has developed a concept of themselves which values a certain degree of autonomy. Adults have a need to be perceived as self directing. The deepest need an adult has is to be treated as an adult, to be treated as a self directing person, to be treated with respect.

2. In terms of their experience. Whereas a child defines his or her self identity by reference to their family, school, community etc. Adults usually define themselves in terms of their experiences. Self identity is derived from what we have done. Accordingly adults are very jealous of the worth of our experience and wherever we find people devaluing our experience, not paying attention to it, not incorporating it in the education plan, we feel rejected as people.

3. In terms of their time perspective. Whereas in most aspects of life, a child's time perspective is one of immediacy they find it hard to postpone the satisfaction of present desires, an adult is more accustomed to postponing immediate satisfactions. But in regard to learning, the time perspectives of children and adults is reversed. Children become used to learning things that will not have immediate application, but will be accumulated into a reservoir of knowledge and skills that will/may be useful in adult life. But an adult's perspective in regard to learning is likely to be one of immediate application. According to Knowles the reason an adult enters into education is to be able to better deal with some life problem about which they feel inadequate now.

Knowles refers to the approach of teaching children as pedagogy and says that the teaching of adults should be based on a different approach which he calls andragogy. Andragogy should take account of the differences outlined above.

APPROACHES TO LEARNING

Honey and Mumford (eg 2000) identified four different approaches to learning. These are not to be confused with the four different learning styles – also developed by Honey and Mumford.

The Intuitive Approach

This involves learning through experience, but not through a conscious process. The person using the intuitive approach claims that learning is an inevitable consequence of having experiences. If questioned they are able to talk in detail about a variety of different experiences, describing what happened and what was achieved. The learning or developmental aspects are rarely, if ever, referred to. A person using the intuitive approach therefore finds it difficult to articulate what they have learnt or how they have learnt it. They are content that learning occurs through some 'natural' process of osmosis.

People who adopt the intuitive approach to learning are likely to say they have been to the "University of Life".

Since people using this approach put their trust in learning as a 'natural' effortless process, they find it difficult to accept that there are advantages to be gained by making the process more deliberate and conscious, either for themselves or for other people.

The Incidental Approach

This involves learning by chance from activities that jolt an individual into carrying out a 'post mortem'. Mishaps and frustrations often provide the spur.

When something hits people using the incidental approach, they are inclined to mull over what happened in an informal unstructured way. They may do this in odd moments such as travelling between appointments, driving home from work, or even sitting in the bath. People using incidental learning tend to use the benefit of hindsight as a way of rationalising what happened.

People using the incidental approach often find it easier to conduct their post mortems by talking things over with someone else, preferably someone who was also present during the experience in question.

The Retrospective Approach

This involves learning from experience by looking back over what happened and reaching conclusions about it. In common with the incidental approach, the retrospective approach is especially provoked by mishaps and mistakes. In addition, however, people using this approach are more inclined to draw lessons from routine events and successes. They therefore extract learning from a diverse range of small and large, positive and negative experiences.

People using the retrospective approach conduct reviews, sometimes in their heads, sometimes in conversation and sometimes on paper. The sequence, slowed down, looks something like:

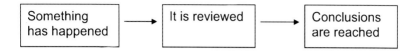

The Prospective Approach

This involves all the retrospective elements, but includes an additional dimension. Whereas retrospection concentrates on reviewing what happened after an experience, the prospective approach includes planning to learn before an experience. Future events are seen not merely as things to be done, but are viewed as learning opportunities.

The sequence in prospective learning is:

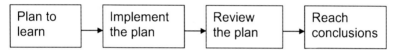

With the increasing professionalisation of social care, the prospective approach is being actively encouraged – it is often referred to as being proactive about your own learning. Increasingly, staff are asked to highlight their learning needs – either before accessing training or in their personal development reviews etc.

LEARNING STYLES

Honey and Mumford have also developed the idea that people have different learning styles. They identified four different learning styles and designed a questionnaire which can be used for people to work out their style.

Activists

Activists are open minded and enthusiastic. They like new experiences and to get involved in the here and now. They are the kind of people who like to "get stuck in". They learn by doing. Activists can get bored once the activity stops and they prefer to look for the next experience rather than reflecting on what they have done.

Reflectors

Reflectors like to stand back and ponder things. They think about many different perspectives before acting. Reflectors like to "chew things over" before reaching any conclusions. Reflectors like to observe people, gather information and have plenty of time to think things over. They will learn best if given plenty of time to think about their responses.

Theorists

Theorists are basically logical thinkers. They like to analyse and question and learn in a step by step, logical way. Theorists will question any new learning and try to ensure it makes sense and fits in with their logical approach. Theorists can be perfectionists and can dislike a flippant approach.

Pragmatists

Pragmatists like to try out anything new to see if it works in practice. They like to take a problem solving approach to learning and are the kind of people who will try and apply something new that they have learnt straight away. If it doesn't work, they won't try it again!

DISSONANCE

Cognitive dissonance was first written about in the 1950s by a psychologist named Leon Festinger (1957). It is used as a theory in a range of ways to understand peoples behaviour, but it is most helpful as a theory of adult learning. The model is depicted below:

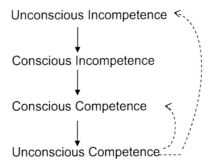

The idea is that when we are called upon to learn something, say a new task, we all start in a position of being unconsciously incompetent – this is sometimes referred to as blissful ignorance. Basically the idea is that we don't know what we don't know! As we begin to learn the new task, we become aware of what we don't know. We are now conscious of our incompetence! This is a very uncomfortable time for most people – after all we are socialised to believe that there is "no such word as can't". Because it's an uncomfortable time, people can give up trying to learn the new task – avoiding the discomfort feels better than dealing with it. However, if people do stick with it and learn the new skill, they will move to the next stage of 'conscious competence.' The person can now do the task but they are very aware of it and very "conscious". If you have learnt to drive, you will probably recognise this phase – when you pulled away you probably said "mirror, signal, manoeuvre" if not out loud, certainly in your head.

Once we become familiar with a task, we move onto being "unconsciously competent" – the task is so familiar we do it on "automatic pilot". The danger here is that people can slip into bad habits and not notice – they may go back to being "unconsciously incompetent". They are now doing the task badly or wrong but they are blissfully unaware. To return to the analogy of driving – most of us probably wouldn't pass our test if we sat it now. This means it is vital to keep alert about what we do and how we do it – which is where reflective practice comes in.

A young woman, Marilia, has recently started working at an older people's care home. Marilia is asked to support Mr Towland. Although she knows his routine, she is a little anxious - Mr Towland has already said he dislikes new staff and young people.

Mr Towland needs help with having a shave. Marilia finds operating the electric razor difficult and the man complains, get angry and shouts. From then on Marilia tries to avoid having to assist Mr Towland in the morning.

An experienced colleague, Frances, becomes aware of this. Frances and Marilia agree to support Mr Towland together for

> a few mornings. Frances shows Marilia how Mr Towland prefers to be shaved. As a result, Marilia is able to assist Mr Towland without Frances' help.

REFLECTIVE PRACTICE

There are two types of reflection –

- Reflection **IN** action
- Reflection **ON** action

(Schon 1987)

Reflection in Action

Reflection IN action is the process of reflection when you are working. Essentially it is working and being aware of what you are doing at the same time. Reflection in action involves:

- Thinking ahead *(Right if that's happened, then I need to .....")*
- Being critical *("That didn't work very well....")*
- Storing up experiences for the future *("I could have dealt with that better, next time I will try....")*
- Analysing what is happening *("She's saying that to test me – I think I should....")*

Reflection in action is happening all the time – if your mind is on the job! We all know people who are planning their night out whilst carrying out a task and would all agree that this doesn't constitute good practice. Having your mind on the job is important. Not only is it good practice but it constitutes reflection in action.

Whilst reflection in action is good practice and can help people to develop their practice, it does have drawbacks. The main problems with reflection in action are:

- You can only see things from your own perspective *("I think, I feel, I'm not sure....")*
- You will only have short term reflection. If your mind is on the job, when the job changes so will your thoughts.

You can address these drawbacks by making sure that you also use reflection ON action.

copyright© Kirwin Maclean Associates

Reflection on Action

This is the reflecting you do after an event. Reflection ON action refers to the process of thinking through and perhaps discussing the incident with a colleague or a supervisor.

Reflection on action is free from urgency and any pressures of the actual event. As such it allows for longer term reflection. You can also ensure that by seeking feedback you use other people's perspectives in your reflection.

The main drawback of reflection on action is that because of time constraints we tend only to think in this way about more complex or critical work issues. Therefore in terms of more routine events and work practice, we tend only to "reflect in action". This can lead us to not making much improvement in our routine work practice. It is important therefore to plan reflection on action to ensure that it covers every aspect of practice.

Planning to reflect rather than simply doing so when something has gone wrong or been particularly difficult, is best practice. Planning to reflect, along with reflection in action and some spontaneous (or unplanned) reflection on action constitutes reflective practice.

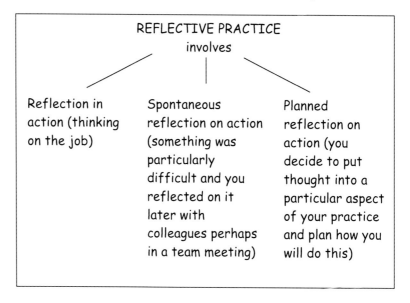

REFLECTIVE PRACTICE
involves

| Reflection in action (thinking on the job) | Spontaneous reflection on action (something was particularly difficult and you reflected on it later with colleagues perhaps in a team meeting) | Planned reflection on action (you decide to put thought into a particular aspect of your practice and plan how you will do this) |

Roth (1989) summarised the basic elements of a reflective process as follows:

- Keeping an open mind about what, why and how we do things
- Awareness of what, why and how we do things
- Questioning what, why and how we do things
- Asking what, why and how other people do things
- Generating choices, options and possibilities
- Comparing and contrasting results
- Seeking to understand underlying mechanisms and rationales
- Viewing our activities and results from various perspectives
- Asking "What if....?"
- Seeking feedback and other peoples ideas and viewpoints

David lived in a service for adults with learning disabilities. He had a severe learning disability and some verbal communication skills but limited vocabulary. David's girlfriend was Rose; she lived in another house and they saw each other regularly.

One evening David and the deputy manager got into a dispute. After the argument, David was quiet. Then he started to tearfully say that Rose didn't love him. The deputy manager assured David that Rose did love him since Rose said so every time Rose and David meet.

Later a colleague, Lottie, who had seen the evenings events thought that David was not saying "Rose doesn't love him!" but that "Nobody loves me." (Due to the argument he felt no-one cared for him.) Lottie shared her thoughts with the team and asked for their thoughts.

A NOTE FOR NVQ and SVQ CANDIDATES AND ASSESSORS

The health and social care NVQ and SVQ Standards refer to theory in most units. You will be able to use this book to support your work on an NVQ or SVQ in a range of ways:

1. Most units refer to theories in relation to certain areas. For example, the following list is recurring in the standards:

    - human growth and development
    - identity and self esteem
    - loss and change
    - power
    - stress and distress

    These themes are covered in the book, as demonstrated on the contents list.

2. You will find that certain units will relate to specific sections of this book. For example, the theories which relate to Unit 33 "Reflect on and Develop Your Practice" are covered in Section Seven: Adult Learning. Some units relate to very specific areas of practice which will be covered in parts of Section Six: Approaches to Care. For example, Unit 393 "Prepare, implement and evaluate agreed therapeutic group activities" will be covered in the groupwork part of this section.

3. There will be certain theories that you need to understand in terms of the specific service user group or setting your work in. For example, if you work with people with learning disabilities, you need to understand social role valorisation, if you work with people with mental health problems you need to understand the recovery model, if you work with children you need to understand attachment etc.

So this book should help you to develop the theoretical knowledge you need to complete the NVQ or SVQ in a range of ways. Choose the best way for you!

REFERENCES

Ainsworth, M., Blehar, M., Waters, E. and Wall, S. (1978) *Patterns of Attachment: A Psychological Study of the Study of the Strange Situation* (Hillsdale) Erlbaum Associates.

Ali, Z. (2001) *Pica in people with intellectual disability: a literature review of aetiology, epidemiology and complications. Journal of Intellectual and Developmental Disability.* 26, 205-215pp.

Argyle, M. (1969) *Social Interaction* (London) Tavistock.

Bandura, A. (1977) *Social Learning Theory* (Englewood Cliffs, New Hersey) Prentice Hall.

Belsky, J. and Cassidy, J. (1994) *Attachment: Theory and Evidence.* In M. Rutter and D. Hays (Eds) *Development Through Life: A Handbook for Clinicians* (373-492pp) (Oxford) Blackwell Scientific Publications.

Bowlby, J. (1969) *Attachment and Loss, Volume I. Attachment* (London) Hogarth Press

Bowlby, J. (1973) *Attachment and Loss, Volume II. Separation: Anxiety and Anger* (New York) Basic Books

Bowlby, J. (1980) *Attachment and Loss, Volume III. Loss: Sadness and Depressions* (New York) Basic Books

Dalrymple, J. and Burke, B. (1995) *Anti-Oppressive Practice: Social Care and the Law.* Open University Press.

Dutt, R. and Phillips, M. (2000) in *Department of Health Assessing Children in Need and their Families* (London) Department of Health.

Erikson, E. (1950) *Childhood and Society* (New York) Norton.

Festinger, L. (1957) *A Theory of Cognitive Dissonance* (Stanford) Standford University Press.

Giddens, A. (1991) *The Reference Project of Self.*

Honey, P. and Mumford, A. (2000) *The Learning Style Helpers Guide* (Maidenhead) Peter Honey Publications Limited.

Healthcare Commission (2006) *Joint Investigation Into the Provision of Services for People with Learning Disabilities at Cornwall Partnership NHS Trust.* (London) Healthcare Commission.

Howe, D., Dooley, T. and Hinings, D. (2000) *Assessment and decision making in a case of child neglect and abuse using an attachment perspective.* Child and Family Social Work, 5, 143-155pp

Inner London Probation Service (1993) *Working with Difference: A Positive and Practical Guide to Anti-Discriminatory Practice Teaching.* (London) Inner London Probation Service.

Knowles, M. (1984) *The Adult Learner: A Neglected Species* (Houston) Gulf Publishing.

Kolb, D.A. (1984) *Experiential Learning.* (Englewood Cliffs, NJ) Prentice Hall.

Kubler Ross, E. (1969) *On Death and Dying* (New York) Macmillan.

Maslow, A. (1970) *Motivation and Personality* (New York) Harper Collins.

McGee, J.J. (1985) *Gentle Teaching.* Paper presented to the annual conference of the New Zealand Association of Teachers of the Mentally Handicapped, Christchurch, New Zealand.

McGee, J.J. (1992) *Gentle teaching assumptions and paradigm.* Journal of Applied Behaviour Analysis, 25, 869-872pp.

Morris. J, (1989) *Able Lives: Women's Experience of Paralysis.* (London) The Women's Press.

Mudford, O. (1995) *Review of the gentle teaching data.* American Journal on Mental Retardation, 99, 345-355pp

O'Brien, J. (1980) *An Ordinary Life* (London) Kings Fund Centre.

Oliver-Kneafsey, K. (2003) *Guidelines for Schools in Understanding and Managing Children with Attachment Disorders* Internet).

Piaget, J. (1928) *Judgement and Reasoning in the Child* (London) Routledge and Kegan Paul.

Philipson, J. (1992) *Practising Equality: Men, Women and Social Work* (London) CCETSW.

Raven, N. (1993) *The bases of power: origins and recent developments.* Journal of Social Issues, 49, 227-251pp.

Roth, R. (1989) *Preparing the reflective practitioner: Transforming the apprentice through the dialectic.* Journal of Teacher Education, 40, 31-35pp.

Rutter, M. (1995) *Clinical Implications of Attachment Concepts: Retrospect and Prospect.* Journal of Child Pschology and Psychiatry. 36 549-571pp.

Ryan, T. and Walker, R. (1999) *Life Story Work* (London) BAAF

Schon, D. (1987) *Educating The Reflective Practitioner* (San Francisco) Jossey Bass.

Skinner, B.F. (1971) *Beyond Freedom and Dignity* (Indianapolis) Hackett Publishing Company.

Thompson, N. (1998) *Promoting Equality* (Basingstoke) Macmillan.

Tuckman, B. (1965) *Developmental Sequence in Small Groups* Psychological Bulletin, 64, 384-399pp. Web link: http://dennislearningcenter.osu.edu/references/GROUP%20DEV%20 ARTICLE.doc (Accessed September 2006)

Tuckman, B. and Jensen, M. (1977) *Stages of small group development revisted.* Group and Organisational Studies, 2, 419-427pp

Vygotsky, L., Vygotskii, L. and Kozulin, A (Eds) (1934/1986) *Thought and Language* (Cambridge, Massachusetts) The MIT Press

Wolfensberger, W. (1972) *The Principle of Normalisation in Human Services.* (Toronto) National Institute on Mental Retardation.

Wolfensberger, W. (1983) *Social role valorization: A proposed new term for the principle of normalization.* Mental Retardation, 21, 234-239pp.

Wolfensberger, W. and Thomas, S. (1983) *PASSING (Program Analysis of Service Systems' Implementation of Normalization Goals): Normalization criteria and ratings manual* (Toronto) National Institute on Mental Retardation.

Zubin, J. and Spring, B. (1977) *Vulnerability – a new view of schizophrenia.* Journal of Abnormal Pschology. 86, 103-124pp.

INDEX